BRITAIN IN OLD P

East Devon

PEOPLE & PLACES

TED GOSLING

SUTTON PUBLISHING

Sutton Publishing Limited
Phoenix Mill · Thrupp · Stroud
Gloucestershire · GL5 2BU

First published 2002

Title page photograph: Empire Day
celebrations in Colyton market place,
c. 1910. (*Ted Gosling Collection*)

British Library Cataloguing in Publication Data
A catalogue record for this book is available from the
British Library.

ISBN 0-7509-2827-1

Typeset in 10.5/13.5 Photina.
Typesetting and origination by
Sutton Publishing Limited.
Printed and bound in England by
J.H. Haynes & Co. Ltd, Sparkford.

During the spring of 1989, the residents of the Ancient Borough of Colyford were opposed to a proposal by Bovis Homes to build luxury houses in the grounds of Kingsholme. Formerly home to the Hollingworth family, Kingsholme was built at the beginning of the twentieth century and was a house of considerable charm. Despite the many objections, Kingsholme, seen here in January 1989, was demolished. The development that followed on the 4-acre site met no local need and extended the village of Colyford further into the countryside. (Express & Echo)

CONTENTS

Dedicated to the staff,
past and present, of
that exceptionally fine newspaper
the Express and Echo

Ye Olde Saddlers Arms, Lympstone, 1959. (Express & Echo)

INTRODUCTION

East Devon has its own character and its natural features have a different beauty from the other parts of the county of Devon. The great rolling hills, the wild seas, the large estuaries, the colourful landscape – these all remain unspoilt and their charm will not change with time. Designated almost entirely an Area of Outstanding Natural Beauty, it is one of the loveliest parts of England. Stretching from the Dorset border to the Exe estuary, and inland as far as the busy M5, much of the holiday traffic passes it by on its relentless drive to Exeter and beyond.

This book highlights the many villages that are often hidden in the steep combes, approached by pretty winding lanes with high banks and hedges lined with a profusion of wild flowers. While East Devon remains a largely unaltered area with a rich history, the aim of this book is to create a pictorial record of the present and the past, and is a welcome addition to this popular series of illustrated titles covering the counties of Devon and Dorset.

Ted Gosling is a master at assembling such magnificent collections of photographs of the area, and in this book he takes us on a nostalgic trip to a host of interesting places such as the seaside towns of Sidmouth, Seaton and Beer, Budleigh Salterton and Exmouth, as well as the inland towns of Honiton, Axminster, Ottery St Mary and Colyton, intertwined with the numerous picturesque villages, all with their own attractive buildings, past characters and unique backgrounds. He illustrates the buildings, farms and churches that have hardly changed over the centuries. Ted is a native of the area, and he has based this title on the vast collection of photographs he has built up over many years. He is the curator and secretary of the Axe Valley Heritage Association, and his annual exhibitions in Seaton, extending over the last fifty years, have complemented his publications about the area.

This latest book cannot fail to interest locals, tourists and anyone who has an association with East Devon.

Roy F. Chapple
Chairman of the Axe Valley Heritage Association
and former East Devon District Councillor

Philip Higginson, the town clerk of Seaton. A Boltonian by birth, his service in the Royal Marines brought him to East Devon in 1961, and he and his family have lived in Talaton since 1973. He describes how he first came into contact with the town: 'My connection with Seaton began in 1972, when I bought my first (and only) new car. It was a yellow VW Beetle (CFJ 271L), and I got to know the town as I took the car to be serviced there at regular intervals. Little was I to know that later on in life I would have a closer connection with what is so aptly described as "the friendly town by the sea". Sadly, the garage is now the site of houses, so often the case in East Devon as the area attempts to meet the demands of those wishing to live in what is a very green and pleasant land. Some confuse development with progress. Unfortunately they are more often than not different, when for the benefit of all they should be synonymous. Fulfilling the needs and desires of an expanding population without destroying the very things which attracted them to move here in the first place, and in the process alienating born and bred Devonians, is a dichotomy not easily reconciled. Unfortunately (or perhaps fortunately) there is no chance to return in a hundred years to see if we got it right.' (*P. Higginson*)

1

The Towns

Aerial view of Seaton, 1957. The changes in the nature of East Devon country life have been immense, and many of the fields that generations of boys from the East Devon towns explored are now housing estates. Although farmers as well as builders can alter the landscape, the impact made by the builders is not reversible. Countless generations must have known and loved the towns of East Devon and would have felt regret at the threat to the green belt surrounding them. Progress must be maintained at a sensible level, but the ever-growing inflow to this area to fuel the economy presents a serious threat to its beauty and amenity. Since this photograph was taken new housing estates have spread out beyond the former boundaries of the town. Although by this time Everest Drive had been completed, the development of land around the cricket field, football field and Harepath Road had not yet taken place. The increase in new housing estates has brought a hundred per cent increase in motor traffic, a pattern repeated throughout East Devon, a pattern which, if continued, will one day destroy for ever the beauty of our countryside. (*Ted Gosling Collection*)

A country scene near Sidmouth, 1901. (*Norman Lambert*)

Temple Street, Sidmouth, 1907. This image of Temple Street on an Edwardian summer day was part of Francis Frith's postcard series. (*Norman Lambert*)

Samuel Good, Seaton's first photographer, took this picture of Fore Street during the summer of 1865. The man on the right, wearing the stove-pipe hat, is clearing out the ditch. He would not have expected his image to survive to the twenty-first century, but it has and it reminds us of how quickly things change. The building on the left, with the tower, is the Sir Walter Trevelyan School, which was designed by Benjamin Woodward and built in 1860. The school was greatly remodelled in the 1960s and lost all but one of its original lancet windows, while the tower over the entrance was reduced in height. (*Seaton Museum*)

Kilmington, *c.* 1900. This is a charming place pleasantly situated on the side of a hill west of Axminster. The church, dedicated to St Giles, was restored in 1861–2, and in the churchyard were the remains of a yew tree said to have been planted to mark the spot where a number of the slain in the Battle of Brunenburgh were buried. This could be legend, but what is fact is that *lobelia urens* grows on Kilmington Hill, one of the few British localities where it can be found. In *Flowers of the Field* by Johns the following description is given: '*lobelia urens* – erect, 12–18 inches high, with a roughish, leafy stem bearing a bracteate raceme of erect purple flowers, very rare, near Axminster, Devon'. (*Ted Gosling Collection*)

Honiton, 6 October 1972. Before the town was by-passed, the long, wide street that runs through the town was on the main London–Exeter road. This High Street, typical of a late Georgian coaching town, features many fine eighteenth-century buildings. Honiton was once an important textile centre, and in medieval times was the third cloth town of Devon. It is known worldwide for its lace, which became especially famous under royal patronage in the nineteenth century. St Paul's Church stands in the centre front and to the left of the church you can see All-Hallows Chapel, used for nearly 300 years as a school-room but now home to the local museum. In the top right-hand corner are the show bungalow and workshops of the Devon Lady cedar wood buildings. Other features in the background include the old school and the car park. (Express & Echo)

This view of Honiton from the west was taken early in January 1982. The high tower in the background, rising more than 100 ft above the town, belongs to St Paul's Church. St Paul's was built between 1835 and 1838 in the Norman style by Charles Fowler. (Express & Echo)

Honiton High Street adorned with flags for George V's Silver Jubilee, 1935. At the close of the twenty-fifth year of his reign the whole country united in what appeared to be one gigantic street party, to thank King George V for the sure guidance he had given to his people. In Honiton the Silver Jubilee in 1935 was celebrated with decorations, a procession to St Paul's Church for a thanksgiving service and other events. (*Ted Gosling Collection*)

The Barn, Fox Holes, Exmouth, *c.* 1907. This house was designed by E.S. Prior following its resurrection after a fire on 4 October 1905. Sir Nikolas Pevsner, one of the most learned and stimulating writers on art and architecture that the twentieth century has produced, described The Barn as 'a brilliant exercise in Art Nouveau domestic design'. (*Ted Gosling Collection*)

The Gardens, Madeira Walk, Exmouth, *c.* 1930. These gardens provided a feast of colour throughout the summer for holiday-makers and residents alike. (*Ted Gosling Collection*)

Exmouth Parade, 10 December 1964. A wet winter's day in December and this was the view looking down The Parade – the shops and buildings seen at the top left were demolished in 1970. (Express & Echo)

Rolle Street, looking up towards Walton's, 12 December 1959. Rolle Street, one of Exmouth's earliest shopping areas, was constructed between 1863 and 1875. Thorntons Chocolates and the New Look fashion shop now occupy the Walton's site, and Sue's Pantry is opposite. The estate agents Meadows & Co. are still operating from their office and R.R. Jeffery's remains a chemists, although it is now operated by a different firm. (Express & Echo)

Exmouth central re-development site, 16 February 1978. The photograph above gives a bird's-eye view of the Exmouth re-development site, which was then due to open for trading in 1979. The project, which cost £1 million, provided a pedestrian precinct with canopied pavements and shops. The venture was designed to rejuvenate the area, which suffered damage during the Second World War. This photograph was taken from a crane towering 100 ft above the site, and comes from the *Express & Echo* library. The shopping centre was named the Magnolia Centre, and was officially opened by television celebrity Angela Rippon on 30 May 1979. In the photograph below, Miss Rippon can be seen performing the opening ceremony, with East Devon District Council chairman Ted Pinney. (Express & Echo)

The arrival of the railway to Exmouth in 1861 transformed the town, making it a Mecca for holiday-makers. A new road was made, which brought the beach closer to the town and was later named Carlton Hill. The photograph above shows Carlton Hill looking towards the sea, from Salterton Road, *c.* 1897. The photograph below was taken in the 1960s and shows that many changes have taken place in the ensuing years. The road is much wider now and the mode of transport has certainly changed. (*Seaton Museum*)

A bustling scene on the Exmouth Parade, 14 December 1961. With only ten days to Christmas, the absence of any festive decorations is most noticeable. The cars are typical of that period and a wintery sun appears to have caught the shoppers outside Woolworth's. (Express & Echo)

This seagull's-eye-view of Exmouth was taken on an early autumn day during the 1960s. Exmouth is the one spot along the East Devon coast blessed with sand, which extends for nearly 2 miles, and makes the town the perfect resort for holiday-makers. Here the popular end of the beach is seen, with The Pavilion and The Beacon behind. (Express & Echo)

Sailors on Exmouth beach with the Royal Beacon Hotel in the background, *c.* 1979. Local waters and conditions create a variety of problems for the yachtsman and sailing by its nature attracts a special breed of person – an individualist with a great love of the sea.

A wet day in Rolle Street, Exmouth, 14 December 1961. An Austin A30, followed by a Vespa scooter, gives this photograph a flavour of the early 1960s. The radio and sports shop of Lawes, on the left, still trades from these premises. (Express & Echo)

Fortfield Terrace, Sidmouth, was constructed in 1795 on the west side of the town to face the sea. This picture of about 1876 was taken by the noted topographical photographer Francis Bedford (1816–94). He produced good images of landscape scenes and travelled through the West Country. The balconies on Fortfield Terrace were at this time a recent addition, and photographs taken in the 1860s show Fortfield Terrace before they were added and the whole row faced. Grand Duchess Helena, sister-in-law to the Czar of Russia, stayed at 8 Fortfield. Her visit is commemorated by the double-headed eagle in the pediment of the terrace. (*Ted Gosling Collection*)

The premises of E. Culverwell & Sons, Fore Street, Sidmouth, *c*. 1902. The Culverwell family was famous for its long association with the *Sidmouth Herald*, which had spanned many generations. The newspaper was first published as *Harvey's Sidmouth Directory* in 1849. When the Culverwell family owned it the title changed to the *Sidmouth Directory* and then the *General Advertiser*. This building was formerly known as the Herald office, and this town-centre premises is now a newsagent's shop. The windows are crammed full of what have become valuable and much sought-after Edwardian children's games and other knick-knacks, including an advertisement for the new game of Diabolo. Diabolo comprised a double-headed spinning top, which was thrown up and caught by means of a string attached to two sticks and was very popular with children before the First World War. (*Ted Gosling Collection*)

Opposite, below: The mill dam, Sidmouth, showing the entrance to the mill leat, *c*. 1875. This early photograph was published by M.M. Cockburn of Bishopston, Bristol, and was no. 354 from a West Country series. The mill dam was built in 1801 to feed a leat that took water down under Salcombe Road to Hooks Mill. This mill ground flour, and the splash of water with the turning of the wheel was one of the delights of early Sidmouth. (*Ted Gosling Collection*)

The Manor Hall, Sidmouth, *c.* 1905. John Edmund Heugh Balfour inherited the manor of Sidmouth and was the town's last lord of the manor. He was born on 22 January 1863 and died in October 1952. He served with the 11th Hussars between 1884 and 1892, and in South Africa during the Boer War between 1899 and 1900, where he was mentioned in dispatches and was awarded a medal with six clasps and a DSO. He was twice mentioned in dispatches in the First World War and received the CMG in 1918, rising in rank and honour to become Col J.E.H. Balfour CMG, DSO. He was a benefactor to Sidmouth in many ways and also built the Manor Hall seen here. (*Norman Lambert*)

Early in the twentieth century an unknown photographer successfully captured the feeling of Edwardian England in this picture of Sidmouth High Street, *c.* 1905. (*Norman Lambert*)

A Sidmouth Motor Company bus, *c.* 1936. This is one of the famous Austin coaches, affectionately nick-named the 'toast rack', that was operated by Dagworthy's. This firm took passengers between Peak and Salcombe Hills every half hour during the summer months. (*Norman Lambert*)

Pikes Court, Sidmouth, *c.* 1920. This row of buildings was a feature of old Sidmouth that disappeared, with other cottages in the High Street, to make way for the gas showrooms. Pikes Court entrance was through an alley between cottages in High Street, and at one time Elizabeth Denner, a pillow-lace maker, lived there. She used to sit outside her front door fashioning lace. (*Norman Lambert*)

The cricket field, Sidmouth, 1907. The first cricket club was established in Sidmouth in 1823 and it played on the present cricket ground, which was then enclosed. Anna Sutton described the ground in her book *A Story of Sidmouth*, 1953: 'Sidmouth has the finest cricket ground in the county. Standing in an elevated position with an uninterrupted view of the Bay to the south, surrounded by fine buildings and beautiful scenery in the background, with well-kept tennis courts, it is unparalleled.' (*Norman Lambert*)

River Sid and Alma Bridge, 2000. The Battle of Alma took place on 20 September 1854 during the Crimean War. The news of the victory caused strong feeling in England: 2,000 men were lost in 2 hours of fighting, including 26 officers. The bridge constructed over the River Sid in 1855 was named after this battle, although the one seen here is the second structure. In 1900 the Urban District Council replaced the original bridge because it was poorly built. At the present time a 'Save Alma Bridge' group is striving to make a case for urgent coastal protection work to be carried out to safeguard this key link on the South West coast path. (*S. Luxton*)

An aerial view of the old market town of Ottery St Mary, which lies peacefully in the heart of the East Devon countryside, November 1972. The town is famous for two things – a church and a poet. The Church of St Mary can be seen in the foreground, looking like a miniature cathedral, which was the intention of Bishop Grandisson of Exeter when he transformed the existing church into a smaller version of Exeter Cathedral for his college of canons. The royal licence for the founding of the college at Ottery St Mary was granted by Edward III on 15 December 1337, and on Christmas Eve Bishop Grandisson presented the church to the warden and canons of his new foundation. The church is full of notable features, which include a fourteenth-century clock, still ticking away after nearly seven centuries. The poet of Ottery St Mary is Samuel Taylor Coleridge (1772–1834), who was born in the town and was the son of John Coleridge, the vicar of Ottery and master of the grammar school. He was, perhaps, the greatest literary genius that came from Devon, yet Ottery St Mary seems to make little of him. (Express & Echo)

Seaton photographed by Francis Frith (1822–98) during the summer of 1907. The drinking fountain in the foreground was given to the town by Mr Willans to mark the Diamond Jubilee of Queen Victoria in 1897, and it was destroyed just before the Second World War. Built by George Henry Richards, the Westleigh Hotel, with its impressive tower detail, stands on the right of Sea Hill. The house on the left was named Seafield, and this was destroyed by a German bomber in the Second World War. How handsome the town looked then, long before it was spoiled by late twentieth-century hands. (*Ted Gosling Collection*)

Opposite, above: Looking down Silver Street, Ottery St Mary, 1977. The red-brick memorial seen in the foreground was erected to commemorate Queen Victoria's Diamond Jubilee in 1897. It is said to be a replica of one of the gate-posts at the entrance to Kensington Gardens. This site was once well known to all of the town's wrong-doers as it was formerly occupied by the town stocks. (Express & Echo)

Opposite, below: Fore Street, Seaton, *c.* 1900. Views like this of people and houses that no longer exist seem to be inherently magical. In them the vanished past is made present again, yet the sense of the passage of time is overwhelming and we are reminded in pictures like this of how quickly things change. The Tudor cottage, on the right in the foreground, is still standing, but the large barn-like building in the background has long gone. This was once a farm building, but at the time of this photograph was used by the Beer Stone Company. (*Ted Gosling Collection*)

Seaton's distorted circle, called The Square, August 1961. At that time Boots occupied the corner site next to The George, and the chemist shop of Hinton Lake & Son was in the premises now owned by Byrne Jones. The Seaton Post Office was next door to Hinton Lake's, and you can see the old-style red telephone box outside the Post Office. The Midland Bank – now HSBC – still occupies the same position next to the Post Office that it did back in 1961. The most interesting feature in this photograph is the archway into The Grove on the right. This was a small part of medieval Seaton and, like Bacon's Barn in Barnards Hill, was swiftly knocked down by developers with no interest in the past. Often old photographs appear to distort a scene, but The Square seemed more attractive then. (Express & Echo)

Fore Street, Seaton, 1936. Next to Edgar Smith's Cycle Works was Smith's Library and Newsagency. The library was the largest circulating library in the district, and the shop also included the first radio department in Seaton. This was run by another member of the family, Vernon Smith, who was an expert in that new medium called wireless. Further up Fore Street you notice Smedley's Central Garage, while in the top right-hand corner of the picture you can see what was once one of Seaton's most famous landmarks – Beever's Clock. Mr C. Beever had a jeweller's shop, and the clock that hung above his showroom window kept the best time in the town, hence that old Seaton saying 'Beever's time'. (*Ted Gosling Collection*)

Many changes have taken place in Seaton's Fore Street since that summer day in August 1962 when the Ford 8 car seen here was caught by the camera manoeuvring between the mini and the delivery van. One of Seaton's most conspicuous landmarks, the Golden Lion pub sign, was relegated, with the pub, to history some years ago. The Cookery Nook Café, seen on the left, is now an estate agency, the shoe shop next to the mini is now a florist's, Carr and Quick's off-licence is long gone and Fore Street has become a semi-pedestrian, one-way only road. (Express & Echo)

Queen Street, Seaton, 1903. The imposing building on the right was once known as Brick House, so named because when it was built in 1824 it was one of the first houses in the town to be constructed with bricks. During the 1890s it became the Freidheim Seaside School for Girls, but by 1903 it was called Montpellier School. Later still it became Ferris and Prescott, the drapers, and at the present time a part of the building houses the local police station. Manor Court now stands on the land behind the iron railings, and to the left of the photograph are the branches of what was a fine, mature copper beech tree. It really was a beautiful tree, especially during the summer months, but it became a casualty of progress when Manor Court was built. (*Ted Gosling Collection*)

Buildings in the ancient town of Colyton are grouped around the Parish Church of St Andrew, a large and very handsome building. The upper part of the imposing tower of the church, with its octagonal lantern, dates from the fifteenth century, with thirteenth-century work at the bottom. The chancel is thirteenth century and much of the rest of the structure is chiefly fifteenth and early sixteenth century. Disaster struck in October 1933 when a fire gutted the nave and aisles. Happily the restorers knew their job and the grand old church was fully restored to its former glory. In the photograph above, Colyton church is seen in 1899. In the photograph below, the interior of the church is seen with splendid candelabra. (*Ted Gosling Collection*)

The Old Court House, Colyton, *c.* 1968. The Old Court House in Queens Square dates from the late fifteenth century, and many fascinating stories surround it. Although it is claimed that it was once a base for Judge Jefferies during his Bloody Assizes, this is more legend than fact. No mention is made of the Court House in the standard work on the Monmouth Rebellion, *The Life, Progresses and Rebellion of James, Duke of Monmouth* by George Roberts, 1844, nor indeed in the book by W. MacDonald Wigfield MA, *The Monmouth Rebellion*, 1985. What is certain is that the men of Colyton were an unruly crowd, and over 100 of them joined the rebel army and were tried at various assizes. Many of them were transported to Barbados and Jamaica, which today might be considered pretty good places to serve out your sentence. (Express & Echo)

A charming photograph of Colyton Chantry Bridge, taken by Francis Frith in about 1890. (*Ted Gosling Collection*)

Axminster Market, Trinity Square, *c.* 1903. This weekly market was where East Devon farmers met to buy and sell and chat about farming. It is still held in Axminster, although no longer in Trinity Square, having moved to South Street in 1912. (*Norman Lambert*)

A wonderfully evocative photograph looking up Castle Hill, Axminster, taken by Kenneth Harman-Young during September 1904. The children seen here are charming, and the street was then a place where they could play in safety. (*Daphne Harman-Young*)

Western Road, Axminster, *c.* 1924. Although there are a few cars on the road, this main route into the town was still a place of marvellous serenity compared with today. (*Ted Gosling Collection*)

Axminster Cottage Hospital, Chard Street, 1913. This photograph was taken not long after the hospital was officially opened on 18 June 1912. The main entrance was then in the front of the building, but at a later date this was closed and moved to the rear. The condition of Chard Street looked a little different in those pre-car days. (*Norman Lambert*)

Budleigh Salterton through the trees, looking east, 1935. At the beginning of the nineteenth century Budleigh was no more than a hamlet by the sea, with the town we know today a creation of the past 160 years. The photographer from Friths of Reigate took this picture and captured that strange stillness found in so many of those photographs taken in the 1930s. (*Ted Gosling Collection*)

The Octagon House, Budleigh Salterton, *c.* 1959. Sir John Millais lived for a time at The Octagon, and it was here he painted his famous work *The Boyhood of Ralegh*. The painting, which was exhibited at the Academy of 1870, shows two boys on Budleigh beach, listening enthralled to an old seaman's yarn. One of the boys is Walter Ralegh, and the other Humphrey Gilbert. Ralegh was born 2 miles away at East Budleigh, and may well have spent time on the beach. (*Ted Gosling Collection*)

The mouth of the River Axe, 13 October 1972. The land on the left of the River Axe, with canals intersecting the flat land, is the Seaton Marshes. A part of this low-lying district is below sea level and the Willoughby Bank, now used by the tramway, once kept out the river water from what were salt marshes. This is an area full of interest and delight, for here in these marshy flats lie hidden many secrets of the past. This is a unique area, attracting wildlife in all its forms, certainly an area that should be protected from any form of development. Since this photograph was taken, a new bridge has been built to by-pass the old one. The bridge seen here was made of concrete and was opened in 1877. Before then travellers to and from Axmouth had to cross by ferry, which was worked by an overhead cable system. The ferryman lived in the small house on the right, beside the river. The Racal factory, the large building on the left of the river, was then in full production, but sadly the firm pulled out of Seaton and the premises are currently empty. (*Ted Gosling Collection*)

Townsend Garage, Beer

Cars for Hire

W. L. OBORN, Proprietor

Michelin Stockists

The Leading Garage for Repairs in Beer

MOTOR REPAIRS
PETROL ❧ OILS
WIRELESS

Electrical Fittings and Lamps
Supplied

It was during the 1920s that the motorist and the motor car came into their own in East Devon, with local garages catering for their needs. In the advertisement above, Mr W.L. Oborn, the owner, promotes the services of the Townsend Garage in Beer. He carried out motor and wireless repairs and also sold petrol from the pump, which was quite an innovation in the 1920s. In the advertisement below, Martin & Staddon state that they are motor engineers based in Budleigh Salterton, and are agents for Dodge cars. (*Ted Gosling Collection*)

DODGE BROS. SALES and SERVICE   Telephone **50**

MARTIN & STADDON

Motor Engineers

BUDLEIGH SALTERTON

HIGH CLASS
PRIVATE
HIRE CARS

Dunlop, Michelin
Tyres

OVERHAULS and REPAIRS

2

The Villages

The secret charm of the old village life we so often dream about is reflected in this photograph of Axmouth taken during the 1920s. The smoke curling up out of the distinctive square chimneys on the old thatched cottages, the village dame peering from her door, the small child sitting in the road looking with curiosity at the passing horse and trap – these elements create a calm landscape and settled world. Yet, of course, this is hardly the truth, for even then the lot of the countryman was hard work and poor pay. The cottage he lived in had serious faults, lacking the convenience of a modern drainage system and water had to be carried indoors from a well. Today we have a romantic image of the past, but for most country people this garden of Eden in East Devon was not paradise. (*Ted Gosling Collection*)

Avondale, Combpyne, 1900. East Devon villages were once a cluster of ancient homesteads, formerly the habitations of yeomen who farmed and worked on the land. These people, like their fathers before them, lived in direct contact with the soil and the land was their great benefactor. The latter half of the twentieth century saw a way of village life disappear, with retired people coming to live in new bungalows and refugees from urban life buying up old farmhouses and cottages. New money with metropolitan attitudes transformed many villages into a form of country suburbia – the untidiness that spoke of a working village was lost as the newcomers disciplined their gardens and surrounding areas to enter 'best-kept village' contests. No one with a reflective mind can fail to see that the spirit of these old villages has gone, and with it goes one more joy of life. This photograph seems to be the very embodiment of peace – it reflects a time when the East Devon countryside was at its best. (*Ted Gosling Collection*)

The village of Branscombe, with part of its church dating from the Norman period, is one of the loveliest villages in Devon. In the parish are interesting houses, once the homes of distinguished families. Egge, or Edge, was the home of the Branscombes, a family that produced three sheriffs of Devon and one of Exeter's greatest bishops Walter Bronescombe, who held office between 1258 and 1280. Hole was the ancient abode of the De-la-Holes and Barnells was built by Captain Ewell, Nelson's captain of marines on the *Victory* at Trafalgar. In the photograph above, the delightful Ye Olde Masons Arms reflects the image of what most people expect in a country pub, September 1964. In the photograph below, this scene encapsulates the secret charm of village life – a thatched cottage along the side of the village road, roses around the door and, a little distance away, the tower of the village church. Branscombe church is dedicated to St Winifred, a Bristol saint of the seventh century. (Express & Echo)

Southleigh, *c.* 1899. A scattered village, Southleigh lies among the wooded hills south of the Coly valley, not far from the large Iron Age hill-fort of Blackbury Castle. The workman in this late Victorian photograph appears to have a load of stones in his cart, so he may have been a council worker employed on road repairs. In the background on the left you can just spot the thirteenth-century Church of St Lawrence. (*Norman Lambert*)

Northleigh village, remote among the luxuriant valley scenery of East Devon, is seen here on a quiet day in 1937. The Church of St Giles, built mainly of local flints in the fourteenth century, is on the right of the photograph. A rector of this church during the sixteenth century was John Carpenter who, during his 34-year stay, found time to write tracts that included one composed in 1586 entitled 'A sorrowful song for sinful souls, composed upon the strange and wonderful shaking of the earth, 6 April 1586'. Did this mean that Northleigh had experienced an earthquake that year? (*Norman Lambert*)

A quiet corner in the village of Branscombe, August 1957. The bee-hive-shaped cottage in the foreground is still named, appropriately, Bee Hive Cottage. (Express & Echo)

Musbury, July 1966. This charming village lies on the margin of the Axe Valley, and takes its name from the Iron Age hill-fort that is situated on the hill above Musbury. Before the Reformation Musbury was the property of the Courtenays and belonged to the Drakes afterwards. Ashe House, about 1 mile away to the north, was rebuilt by Sir John Drake, 2nd Bt. in about 1670–80. It is often reported that John Churchill, who became the Duke of Marlborough, was born at Ashe House, but this is most unlikely and it seems more probable that he began his life in Great Trill, in the parish of Axminster. (*Ted Gosling Collection*)

Awliscombe, *c.* 1885. This photograph shows what the roads were like in East Devon before motor traffic. Today the road through the village has become a busy feeder-route to the M5 motorway, but in the late Victorian period it was just a muddy, untarred road. The star of this picture is undoubtedly the fine timber wagon parked at the side of the road. (*Ted Gosling Collection*)

The Smithy, Beacon, Luppitt, *c.* 1902. The extension at the side of the building is the old workshop, inside which is a plaque with the date 1870. The current owners Philip and Sally Twiss say parts of the house date back to the 1780s. The smithy is now named Swallow Cliff and stands at the top of a cul-de-sac, half way along which is the former Blackdown Mission building, just visible in the picture at the end of the lane. (*Ted Gosling Collection*)

Whitford, *c.* 1950. Whitford is an ancient manor in the parish of Shute. Its name in all probability is a form of Wide-ford. In about 1342 a market was granted to a Peter de Brewose, to be held on Wednesday within his manor of Wytteford, and a fair to last four days at the festival of St Peter-ad-Vincula. The manor came to Peter de Brewose from the Sandfords, whose family, through marriage, obtained it from the Bassets. Here, on a quiet summer day in the early 1950s, Whitford appears peaceful, dreaming perhaps of those days long ago. (*Norman Lambert*)

Axmouth village, *c.* 1956. It is sad to think that the cottages on the right are gone, to be replaced with a more modern building. In the early days, the use of local materials was a distinctive feature of East Devon villages and in cottages like this you can find a charm, combined with a feeling that these were once the homes of village ancestors. (*Ted Gosling Collection*)

Taken during the summer of 1956, this Frith photograph gives a view of the traditional countryside of the Axe Valley, with its chequer board of green fields divided by lush hedgerows. The still-unspoilt village of Axmouth, with the square tower of the Church of St Michael, can be seen in the centre, and beyond the marshes of the River Axe. Although present-day Axmouth is a quiet, delightful place, there is much proof of its great antiquity and former importance. In Roman times it was the southern terminus of the Fosse Way, and in the Saxon occupation of the seventh century it was one of the earliest villages to be founded. It belonged to King Athelstan, later to Edward the Confessor and then to William I. Leland described Axmouth as 'an old and bigge fischar toune', and it was certainly much larger than it is today. The River Axe was considerably wider during the Roman period, and at Axmouth it was about half a mile wide. The Romans almost definitely formed a harbour here, the site being at the southern end of the Fosse Way and also within a short distance of two Roman villas, Honey Ditches at Seaton and Holcombe at Uplyme. (*Ted Gosling Collection*)

Pear Tree Corner, Colyford, *c.* 1894. Although Colyford itself was not a Roman settlement, the now-busy A3052 that runs through it was once a branch road of the Icknield Way that linked Seaton and the quarries at Beer with the rest of Roman Britain. In the late nineteenth century Colyford was still a peaceful village, but this has now changed radically and quickly. Compare the quiet, untarred road with the same scene today – the houses and wall at the top right have been demolished to improve Pear Tree Corner. This photograph was taken by Francis Frith and at that time it was possible to stand in the middle of the road to get the shot – trying this today would be suicidal. (*Ted Gosling Collection*)

A peaceful scene at Gully Shoot, Colyford, *c.* 1900. This road is now the busy A3052. The area at the bottom of Gully Shoot was known as Bishops Stoke, and at the time of this photograph a Mr Board lived in one of the cottages on the left. Board had a local fish round, and herring could be purchased from him for as little as 1s a dozen. (*Ted Gosling Collection*)

Buyers from all parts of the country attended the auction of the Rousdon Estate, which was held during September 1937. The estate was described as one of the beauty spots of England, and the sale comprised 145 lots, including The Landslip and the village of Rousdon. The Rousdon school house with a cottage and Post Office is pictured here in 1937. The school contained three classrooms, a dining room and a large asphalt playground. The school house was occupied by the headmaster and the adjoining cottage by the district nurse. A single room in the building was used by the village Post Office. At the sale of the Rousdon Estate this property realised £1,700. (*Ted Gosling Collection*)

Opposite, below: The atmosphere of Victorian Axmouth is apparent in this 1885 photograph of the village. East Devon villages were still independent communities at that time, and in some cases were like colonies shut off from the outside world. The man on the left, beside the horse and cart and standing outside the Harbour Inn, and the children on the right were part of a village scene now long gone, where the squire Sanders Stephen Esq. of Stedcombe Manor still ruled and made sure that his tenants were in church on Sunday. (*Ted Gosling Collection*)

Southleigh, *c.* 1901. Life has changed dramatically since the day when an unknown photographer took this shot of the village. This was still an age when country people living in the villages of East Devon lived a restricted rural life, geared to the slow rhythm of the changing seasons. The farm workers winding their way up the road belonged to the vast class of agricultural labourers who, at the time, were the biggest class in East Devon. There are fewer farmers today and modern farming techniques have reduced the need for so much labour. (*Norman Lambert*)

The village of Beer photographed by Francis Frith over a hundred years ago. The monument standing on the plot in front of the Anchor Hotel commemorates the artist Hamilton Macallum, who for many years made Beer his home. When he died in 1896, at the age of fifty-five, this memorial and stone seat were erected by his friends. The thatched cottages to the right of the Anchor were knocked down at a later date and the site is now a car park. Much has changed in Beer since that day long ago, but the village still remains one of the best loved in Devon. (*Ted Gosling Collection*)

Looking down Fore Street in Beer, 1883. For almost fifty years Francis Frith was the most productive landscape photographer in England. Today we recognise that Frith's skill lay in his ability to capture a view of what would soon become a lost landscape. In the 1880s photography was still sufficiently unusual to attract attention, and the few villagers around at the time this picture was taken are looking with interest at the photographer. A great deal has changed since that far-off day and although Beer Brook, the open stream that runs down one side of the village, is still flowing, the thatched cottages on the right were pulled down to make way for the Beach Hotel. (*Ted Gosling Collection*)

The Court Hall and the village of Sidbury photographed by W. Harding Warner in 1875. The village of Sidbury lies in the Sid Valley, and takes its name from the early Iron Age hill-fort to the south-west, known as Sidbury Castle. The Church of St Giles, with its Norman tower, is one of the most interesting in Devon. The Norman chancel was set above an ancient crypt, which was revealed following restoration work in 1898–9. Although the exact date of the crypt is unknown, it is of Saxon origin. The Court Hall, seen on the left, dates from the late sixteenth century and got its name from the time when the judges stayed there on their circuit rounds. The church tower is in the centre background. (*Ted Gosling Collection*)

The Keepers Cottage, Combe Raleigh, *c.* 1900. This house is at the southern tip of Coombe Wood, on Clapper Lane, about a quarter of a mile from Honiton. The present occupiers believe it to be 300 years old, but it is no longer thatched. (*Ted Gosling Collection*)

Shelf House, Luppitt, *c.* 1908. (*Ted Gosling Collection*)

Calhays Farm, *c.* 1910. This farm lies on Mount Stephens, above the village of Luppitt, with breathtaking views of the valley of the River Love. In 1850, Calhays was farmed by Clement Griffin, who was a member of a large family of farmers who at that time lived in Luppitt. By 1883 Joseph Pearn was the occupier, although the farm still belonged to the Griffin family. However, by the First World War it was owned by the Totterdales. I am not sure who the people in the photograph are, but it could be my Great-Uncle James Totterdale and his family. (*Ted Gosling Collection*)

3

The People

Ottery St Mary Urban District Council members, April 1973. Front row, left to right: F.L. Manley, W.R. Hansford, Chairman, W.F. Bennett, Clerk to the Council; middle row: W.A. Murray, Chairman of the Finance and Establishment Committee, W.F. Court, W.F. Westlake, W.G. Hughes, A. Colman, J.F. Godfrey, P.R. Pearce, N.W. Willis, Deputy Clerk; back row: A. Turner, G. Hembury, H.G. Godfrey, W.R. Retter, S.R. Luke, P. Billington, Public Health Inspector, D.S. Burtenshaw, Surveyor, P.B. Rice. (Express & Echo)

Dr Edward Tonge, standing on the left, with his father and family, 14 June 1907. A native of Yorkshire, Dr Tonge came to the Beer practice in 1897, where he remained until his death in 1937. He took a keen and practical interest in the affairs of the village, giving help and encouragement wherever needed, never sparing himself in the cause of others. He lived for his work and, faithful to his self-imposed duty, he left his sick-bed to minister to those whose needs were greater. The care that he gave to the people of Beer endeared him to everyone. His name became synonymous with Beer, and when he died, aged sixty-four, the entire community mourned him. During the First World War he was principal medical officer in charge of the Seaton Auxiliary Hospital, sited at Ryalls Court. He also acted as an Admiralty surgeon. For that work, Dr Tonge was awarded the OBE. He was also a great friend of Beer artist John White and whenever any of White's family needed medical attention, Dr Tonge was paid with a painting. Today, John White's pictures of East Devon range in price from £750 to £8,000, so he made what might be termed a good family investment. (*Ted Gosling Collection*)

This striking image of the Gosney family was taken on 4 May 1863. The photographer remains anonymous, although the style seems to suggest that he was provincial. The little boy standing next to his father was Charles F. Gosney. He became the first chemist in Seaton, and he had his shop in Marine Parade until his death in 1935. Charles was famous for his home-made medicines, such as Gosney's Neuralgic Mixture, Gosney's Bronchial Syrup and Gosney's Corn Cure. You get the impression from his early advertisements that if you had it, Gosney could cure it. (*Seaton Museum*)

Walter John Totterdell, who farmed in the Luppitt area, was born on 12 April 1845. He is seen here with his wife Mary, who was born on 18 September 1848. He has the face of a strong man, a man who understood what farming involved, a man who spent his life working on the land to provide food for his fellow countrymen. He must have been about forty-five years of age when he went down to Honiton with his wife Mary to visit the studio of local photographer Alfred Griffiths to have this cabinet photograph taken. Walter died on 7 May 1931, aged eighty-seven. His wife Mary died on 26 May 1921, aged seventy-seven. (*Ted Gosling Collection*)

Elizabeth Totterdale, born on 4 May 1868, was the eldest daughter of Walter John and Mary Totterdale, who farmed at Luppitt. She married John Gosling in 1892, and this photograph was taken about five years before her wedding day. In this image we see a young woman of the 1880s on the threshold of womanhood. Her beauty was the sort that appealed to the Victorians, serious with nothing sensual about it. Elizabeth had six children and died aged ninety. A lifetime member of the Plymouth Brethren, she always had a quiet dignity in her bearing and was much loved by her family. (*Ted Gosling Collection*)

The Revd Herbert Mackworth Drake MA, Otterton, 1906. Drake, who was born on 28 April 1870, was a descendant of the ancient Devon family the Drakes of Ashe House, Musbury. He was educated at Marlborough College and Keble College, Oxford, and was ordained as a deacon in 1893, becoming a priest the following year. He was the acting chaplain with the Devonshire Regiment in South Africa during the Boer War, and was awarded the Queen's and King's South African medals. A brave and much-loved man, he rescued people from drowning in the River Torridge, for which he was presented with the Royal Humane Society's medal in 1897 and clasp in 1898. He became vicar of Otterton near Budleigh Salterton in 1904. He was a member of the St Thomas Board of Guardians and served on the UDC. There are two famous members of the Drakes of Ashe family: the Duke of Marlborough was a descendant on the maternal side; before him, in the early sixteenth century, Bernard Drake was a famous seaman who associated with such prominent sailors as Ralegh, Hawkins and Gilbert. (*Ted Gosling Collection*)

Pride of achievement is seen in the faces of this Colyton football team who won the Morrison Bell and Lyme Regis Hospital cups in the 1924/5 season. Back row, left to right: George White, Reg White, Dan Woodgate, Bill Solway, Donald Baker, Mr Jarvis, Mr Swatridge, Bill Littley, Bill Hooper; middle row: Charlie Facey, Bert Warren, Harry Strawbridge, Ollie Bastable, Mr Ellis; front row: Bert Copp, Georgie Fry, Billy Hann, Wilf White. (*Ted Gosling Collection*)

Clifford Charles Gould was born on 23 April 1866 and in 1895 became one of the first members of the newly formed Seaton Urban District Council. In 1916 he became the council chairman, a position he held until his death in 1939. He held the rare distinction of never having missed a meeting of that authority for twenty-three years. Clifford Gould was a manager of Seaton Trevelyan School from 1900 until 1939. His numerous other appointments included director of the Seaton and District Gas and Coke Co., president of the Seaton Bowling Club, chairman of the Axe Vale Musical and Operatic Society, chairman of the Seaton Horticultural Society and chairman of the Old Age Pensions Committee. He was an outstanding figure in the public life of Seaton for over forty years, a man who lived for the town. (*Seaton Museum*)

St John Ambulance men, looking very smart, attending the dedication of the first motor ambulance in Seaton, *c.* 1938. Originally a Chrysler car belonging to Dr James of the Ryalls Court School, it was given to the town and converted to an ambulance by A. Dowell & Sons, coach-builders, of Exeter. Mr H.F. Norcombe, the war-time chairman of Seaton Council, is seen standing on the left, next to Harry Clapp. The three St John Ambulance men standing against the vehicle were, left to right: Mr Barr, Mr A. Gapper, Mr C. Minhinnett. (*Seaton Museum*)

The local news hawk Alex Alexander, 2001. Based at home on a farm in Luppitt, near Honiton, Mr Alexander covers local news items for Pulman's (some of which have become national headlines), ranging from the sublime to the truly ridiculous. These have included: the reprieve of 'Phoenix', the foot-and-mouth calf they could not cull; the 8-mph flight of a 'hit and run' motorised wheelchair driver who demolished a Seaton shop window; and the closure by Insignia of the village Post Office at Farway, which had been run by the same family for 150 years. Mr Alexander started his career in journalism on the *Baptist Times* denominational newspaper in 1983, before moving to the *South London Guardian*, the *Acton Gazette*, the *Cornish & Devon Post* at Launceston and the *Western Morning News* in Plymouth, where he served as a news editor, crime reporter and farming editor. For five years he also ran his own publishing business before returning to mainstream journalism to help rebuild Pulman's, which almost closed at the end of the 1990s before the arrival of new owners Tindle Newspapers and new editor Philip Evans. (*Alex Alexander*)

Norman Whinfrey, who died in 1998, was a trustee and founder member of the Axe Valley Heritage Association. He retired in 1978 to the East Devon village of Axmouth with his wife Peggy, after thirty-two years in Fleet Street. In 1946 he joined Bradbury Agnew, the publishers of *Punch* and the *Countryman*. His job then was to rebuild the trade connections that had been largely destroyed during the war years. He became publisher in 1956 and the first non-family director, later being appointed managing director. At that time Farming Press became part of the group and three natural history magazines were launched, aimed at various age groups. The Periodical Publishers Association had virtually all magazine publishers in its membership, and he served on many of its committees before becoming chairman of the General Council. After retirement he found more time for his interest in archaeology, and became a member of three archaeological societies. He was very knowledgeable about the Romans and early primitive man, and his lectures for the Axe Valley Heritage Association always filled the hall to overflowing. (*Seaton Museum*)

Photographer Colin Bowerman, 2001. For the past eighteen years Colin Bowerman has been recording the triumphs – and some of the tragedies – of life in East Devon for local newspapers. He trained and qualified as a photographer on the *Maidenhead Advertiser* and became chief photographer there. He then spent six years in Fleet Street with United Newspapers, followed by eighteen months with a news agency in Guildford working for the national newspapers. He then moved to Hemel Hempstead to the Thomson organisation's paper the *Evening Echo*. When that newspaper closed down Colin, with his wife and two daughters, moved to Colyton and joined Pulman's *Weekly News*. Seven years ago he became a freelance photographer and still supplies images to the local newspapers. (*Colin Bowerman*)

Shortly after the outbreak of the Second World War long lines of children could be seen in the cities making their way to the railway station for evacuation to the country. East Devon became a safe haven for hundreds of evacuees, and these included a young Terry Scales, seen here in 1990 working on an oil painting of Deptford Creek. Terry arrived in Seaton in 1940 as an evacuee from South London. His first shock was trying to understand the speech pattern as the locals seemed to converse with strange words, such as 'dasn't', 'casn't', 'thake' and 'girt', closer to James I English than the language he was familiar with. As a seven-year-old he eagerly embraced this brave new world and made many friends among the local boys and girls. One, a fisherman's son, often took him out in the seine boat to bring in the lobster pots. His years in Seaton were one long adventure, and probably the most significant single experience of his life. Being so closely in touch with nature sowed the seeds of his future career, that of a landscape painter. East Devon today remains much as he remembers it, thankfully unscarred by modern development. (*Terry Scales*)

Edwin Spencer, 1918–98. Seaton people were fortunate when, in 1975, Edwin Spencer and his wife Ann decided to come and live in the town, setting up a craft shop. This offered genuine hand-made articles created by individual craftsmen, which was a new and rare phenomenon and made a welcome change from the gaudy souvenirs then available. Edwin Spencer, seen here with Ann in 1975, originally trained as a cabinet-maker. During his final year he produced work that gained an award at the International Exhibition at Brussels in 1935, and he was later chosen to make a cabinet for presentation to HM Queen Mary. He qualified as a teacher, specialising in craftwork, but resigned his post in 1960 and was invited to set up a workshop to carry out repairs on native craftwork. It was then that he had the idea of laminating two or more woods to produce contrasting grain and colour and to create jewellery in laminated exotic woods, examples of which can be seen in the photograph. (*Ann Spencer*)

Brendan Salter, owner of The Seaton residential and nursing home, and Matron Janet Eveson, 1992. The Old Manor nursing home, formerly the Stella Maris Convent School, was rescued from the brink of closure by Brendan Salter in February 1991. Once the home of the creators of the Ever Ready Battery business, the elegant Georgian building has been sympathetically restored over the past decade by Brendan and his wife Heather, retaining its country house atmosphere while providing everything you should expect from a premier care home. The building, which was never a manor house, was renamed The Seaton in 1998 when it became a nursing and residential home in readiness for the twenty-first century. The Seaton offers a first-class service which is a credit to the loyal team of staff, many of whom were employed at its inception as a home. The Seaton is very much an integral part of the town. (*Brendan Salter*)

Julie Rowe (née Payne) participating in the GRIZZLY, 1998. Recently voted by Britain's leading running magazine as the number-one event in the country, the GRIZZLY, organised by the Axe Valley Runners, is also classed as the toughest in Europe. Competitors come from all over Great Britain, France, Germany, Holland and even New Zealand to take part in the event, which starts from Seaton Esplanade and attracts over 2,000 runners. Julie Rowe describes what it feels like to take part: 'Having run both the GRIZZLY and the London Marathon, I would say they are both physically demanding, but in totally different ways. London just goes on and on, albeit on a flat firm surface, whereas with the GRIZZLY there is always another gruelling hill, pebbly beach, knee-deep smelly bog or a cliff at Beer or Branscombe. It's a great event and well organised, but not worth taking on unless you train specifically for the GRIZZLY. Each year the course changes slightly, and it's always more difficult. The course is now in excess of 18 miles and is considered to be one of the UK's toughest off-road races. It is set in beautiful countryside, but when you are so exhausted, the scenery is the last thing on your mind. The only thing you want to see is the FINISH.' (*Julie Rowe*)

The start of the 1992 GRIZZLY. Nearly 700 entrants can be seen on Seaton beach with the cliffs of Beer and Branscombe ahead. (Express & Echo)

Margaret Rogers had holidayed with the family at Branscombe since she was five months old, and she came back with her husband and children, buying a house in 1972 and taking early retirement in 1978. She worked as a graduate history teacher and trained teachers for twenty years, becoming head of education at Maria Grey College, with one year's work at Exeter University. Following her retirement she became very involved with local politics, and served as Liberal councillor for Seaton on East Devon District Council and for Seaton Rural on Devon County Council, later as a Liberal Democrat. She was a very active councillor, presiding over many committees, and was chairman of Devon County Council in 1998–9. She enjoys to the full village life and is active in several local organisations, still working to fulfil her remaining ambitions for the area.
(*Colin Bowerman*)

Colyton historian Miss Pat Goate displaying some of the local artefacts that have been unearthed around Colyton, February 1987. (Express & Echo)

Members of staff at Meadows Estate Agency, Exmouth, 2001. Estate agents play an important role in the property market of East Devon. Although many sold out to insurance companies and building societies in the mid-1980s property boom, it is good to know that some, like Meadows of Exmouth, have remained independent. Meadows was set up in 1922, moving to the existing premises in Rolle Street in 1948. The firm is well established and deals with all property matters, being chartered surveyors as well as estate agents. Currently on the estate agency side partners Viv Woodall and Stuart Burgess are supported by Judy Breckon and Jenny Davis. The residential surveys, commercial valuations, rating, lease and rent reviews and planning advice is carried out by two chartered surveyors, partners Philip Hannah and Malcolm Williams. Secretarial tasks are undertaken by Tracey Clifford-Harding and Rachel Hutchings. The book work is done by Debbie Williams. Meadows also acts for the Clinton Devon Estates, a very large owner within Devon, offering valuation and development advice, together with disposal of surplus farm houses and buildings, mainly by auction. Over the years the nature of the job has changed very little, being a 'people' However, the technology has altered greatly, with computer link-ups and multi-listing of properties with oth together with digital cameras. Seen here, left to right, are: Jenny Davis, Philip Hannah, Stuart Burgess, Clifford-Harding and Viv Woodall. (*Meadows*)

Sheila Luxton (née Nice) has lived in Sidmouth all her life. She was a member of the Sidmouth Post Royal Observer Corps for forty-seven years, until stand-down in 1991. When an episode of the television programme *Jeeves and Wooster* was filmed in Sidmouth, Sheila was lucky enough to be picked as an 'extra'. She is also well known as a beachcomber. At present she is the deputy curator at Sidmouth Museum and is very interested in local history and archaeology. She took part in the excavation of the Roman villa at Holcombe, near Uplyme, between 1969 and 1971. (*S. Luxton*)

Jack Loud, the Seaton milkman, and his milk float, *c.* 1907. Jack Loud lived at Belmont in Fore Street, Seaton, and went from door to door supplying his milk out of the churn into his customers' jugs. In those far-off days milk did not keep very well, and farmers did not pasteurise it. (*Ted Gosling Collection*)

Seaton boys on a youth club outing to Weymouth, *c.* 1952. Left to right: Richard Moore, Don Rodgers, Henry Richards, Fred Cockram, Alan Baker, Richard Way, Arthur Crichard, Gordon Pritchard. (*Ted Gosling Collection*)

Honiton Royal British Legion Cricket Club, *c.* 1960. Back row, left to right: Bill Stone (umpire), Derek Warren, Dennis Rugg, Reg Watts, -?-, Ray Cleaver, John Stoodley; front row: Gerald Bellamy, Barry Pulman, Ken Moore, Les Gollop, Ed Bonneta. (*John Stoodley*)

Honiton Town Football Club, *c.* 1961. Back row, left to right: Derek Evans, Brian Ward, Cyril Pike, John Atkins, Michael Tinham, John Stoodley, David Pike (linesman); front row: Barry Cornwell, Charlie Gratton, Pat Leisk, Dick Collins, Alec Gosling. (*John Stoodley*)

The Bedford Family Hotel, Sidmouth, *c.* 1912. The man outside the hotel on his three-wheel cycle is Theophilus Mortimore, Sidmouth's town crier. He is seen here resplendent in his uniform, a cocked, gold-braided hat, scarlet coat and buckle boots. Theo, with his rich Devon accent, was one of Sidmouth's greatest characters. It was to the Bedford Hotel that the fashionable John Wallis Marine Library was transferred in 1809. (*Norman Lambert*)

Residents of the Ottery St Mary warden-supervised houses, *c.* 1977. The four tenants who wrote to the local council appealing 'please – help us to keep warm this winter' are, left to right: Mrs Kate Stear, Mrs Winifred Crawford, Miss Lily Sparks and Mrs Gladys Bastyan. (Express & Echo)

Axmouth Home Guard, *c.* 1942. The plan to raise Local Defence Volunteers in 1940 met with an immediate response in East Devon. The name was soon changed to the Home Guard, although they were known affectionately as 'Dad's Army'. By the end of 1940 the Home Guard nationally numbered 1.5 million men and during the preparations for D-Day in 1944 they took over most of the security duties on the Home Front. The men from the village of Axmouth played an important part in the Second World War, and after their final muster in 1945 the community expressed immense gratitude to them for all the voluntary work they had done during the difficult days of the war. Those seen here are, back row, left to right: Jeff Puddicombe, Gordon Hunt, Ray Hunt, Leslie Hunt, Mr Mann Sr, Mr Mann Jr; middle row: Herbie Clements, Jack Good, Ted Snell, Jim Cross, Jim Board, Ken Morgan, Mr Mann; front row: Frank Snell, Harry Newbury, Len Weekes, the Revd Swift, Howie Owen, Ken Webber, Victor Worden. (*Ted Gosling Collection*)

Seaton AFC, 1923/4. This club was formed just after the First World War and some of the first players are seen before a match. This fixture, against Axminster, took place on the Colyford Road pitch on Easter Monday 1924 and attracted a large crowd of spectators. Seaton, fielding a strong side, won this match by five goals to three. Players seen here include Walt Lovering, Fritz Miller, Tom Newton, Ralph Rodgers, Nippy Ball and one of the Tolman brothers. (*Ted Gosling Collection*)

Board of directors, Axminster Carpets, *c.* 1969. Axminster is associated to the present day with the famous carpets that bear its name. The original manufacturer was Mr Thomas Whitty, a local man who established a factory here in 1755. The business was carried on until 1835, when the factory was closed and the looms were removed to Wilton. This was a great blow to Axminster, and when Mr Harry Dutfield revived the industry in 1937 he had the support of the whole town. The first carpet was produced that year, the first to be made in Axminster for 102 years. At present the success of Axminsters from Axminster is well known, because of the support of a loyal workforce under the guiding hand of able directors. Left to right: Mr E. Gill, Mr T.N. Duthers, Mr R. Luff, Mr R.M. Laws, Mr N.A. Humphries, Mr W.H. Dutfield, Mr R.J. Wright, Mr S.J. Dutfield, Mr G. Ayres. (*Ted Gosling Collection*)

Opposite, below: Guardians and officials of the Axminster Union outside the workhouse, 31 March 1930. Back row, left to right: E.A. Warnes, H.K. Morrish, O. Allhusen, F.W. Northcote, E.G. Bastaple, H.T. Cligg, A.J. Northcote, D. Slack; second row: E.G. Kirby, E. Shaw, H.M. Thomas, I.M. Warnes, E.E. Bullock, A. Du-Rose, W.E. Taylor, A.H.D. Smith, F.J. Holmes, J.E. Bullock; third row: A.J. Edwards, C. Forward, A.R. Whittington, H. Collier, A.J. White, W.T. Trott, J. Follett, W. Beviss, J.R. Pratt, J. Cowling, W.J. Wright; front row: G.D. Lansley, G. Hurford, the Revd T. Long, Miss E. Allhusen, J. Richards, E.H. Cuming (chairman), G.H. Morrish, H.E.V. Crawford (vice-chairman), C. Gould, A.F. Goddard. (*Ted Gosling Collection*)

The Territorial Army soldiers seen here were camping at Rousdon in the summer months of 1913. During this camp, which lasted for a fortnight, they would have spent their days in drilling, route marching, manoeuvres, finishing with a demonstration of field operations. Little did they realise that in just over one year playing at soldiering for them would be over, and they would be joining the British Expeditionary Force ('The Old Contemptibles') to fight the Kaiser's army, which had invaded Belgium. (*Ted Gosling Collection*)

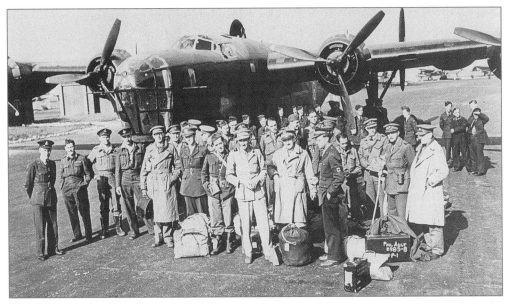

Dunkeswell was home to US Navy Arm Wing 7 and here, in 1944, American airmen from the 1st Navy Squadron pose in front of a Liberator. During the Second World War the Americans made an enormous impact on East Devon. Everywhere, along lanes and in woods, were parked long lines of jeeps, trucks and transporters, covered with camouflage netting, all involved in the build-up for D-Day. (*Seaton Museum*)

Lew Leyman, *c.* 1965. Lewis James Leyman was born at 11 Highwell Road, Seaton, on 2 April 1927. He was the son of Norman and Daisy Leyman, and his grandfather was the well-known James Leyman, one of Seaton's first developers and who built Highwell Road in about 1912. Lew Leyman attended Colyton Grammar School from 1937 to 1943 and prior to joining the Navy in 1945 worked for a firm of chartered accountants. During his service with the Royal Navy he served as a writer on the staff of the Commander-in-Chief, East Indies, at Trincomalee, Ceylon. In November 1947 he joined the old Exeter City police force and served on foot patrol, on motor patrol and on the administration side. Lew was promoted to sergeant in 1960, and also became a member of the Exeter City Police first aid team, which won the Pym Trophy for the National Police Championship five years in succession. Following the formation of the combined Devon and Cornwall constabulary, which included the Exeter City police force, he spent his last four years before retirement in the control room. A quiet and much-respected man, Lew and his wife Dorothy remained in Exeter, and celebrated their golden wedding on 25 August 2001. (*Seaton Museum*)

Exmouth United AFC, 1912/13. This photograph is typical of its time and kind, the players looking proud to be members of this team. (Express & Echo)

George Toogood, who was born at Curscombe, Feniton, in 1835, was a true son of Devon. He had life-long experience as an agriculturist, and when he retired he was the oldest tenant of the Right Hon Sir John Kennaway Bt., MP. Toogood was an exhibitor of cattle at the Exeter Fat Stock Show for many years and officiated as judge on two occasions. He was elected a member of the Honiton Board of Guardians at the age of nineteen, and served on it for thirty-five years. Other services to the community included being a member of the Ottery St Mary Hospital, a knight of the Primrose League and a churchwarden. For twenty-five years he was in the 3rd Battalion DR, and shot for Devon, competing for four years at the Wimbledon International Shooting Competition. George Toogood died in 1907. (*Ted Gosling Collection*)

Opposite, below: This fine 1926 Lancia Lambda was a familiar sight in East Devon during the 1950s. The Du-Pain family, who ran the tea bungalow on Woodbury Common, owned the car, until they sold it to Ted Gosling in 1956 for £75. The Lambda, with a V4 engine of 2.1 litres and a top speed of more than 70 mph, was an advanced car for its time. Independent front suspension, an alloy cylinder block and a unitary body chassis were just a few of the vehicle's features. The car is seen here in the Sidmouth Ham car park in 1959, with Sidmouth resident Ann Irish sitting in the rear. The woman in the driving seat came from Italy and when Ted Gosling informed her that he had a Lancia car, she said, 'Do take me for a ride'. Unfortunately, at that time Italians did not appreciate vintage cars and when she saw the Lambda she collapsed with laughter saying, 'Do you call that heap of old iron a Lancia?' (*Ted Gosling Collection*)

Before the First World War, the Sunday school treat was the main event for children in the East Devon calendar, and the inhabitants of Shute are certainly enjoying their day on 17 June 1909. The teachers are taking tea with members of the Seaton Congregational church. It was the best time of the year, when hay meadows were patterned with wild summer flowers and larks soared and sang. A golden Edwardian summer that would sadly change within a few years when many of the young men who were present would soon be in the hell of such places as Vimy Ridge, Ypres, Somme, Kut and Gallipoli. However, on this happy day that was not only in the future, but beyond their comprehension. (*Seaton Museum*)

Ann Adams moved to Seaton in 1972 and was soon very involved in the affairs of the town. She became a councillor on the Seaton Town Council, serving from 1976 to 1997. During her years of office she served as the chairman during five terms. Ann also brought her experience to the bench when she became a magistrate in 1989. In 1983 Ann purchased Windsor Books in Cross Street, Seaton. Her shop quickly became a centre for local people to go, not only to purchase books, but also to have their problems sorted out by Ann. (*Ann Adams*)

Geoff Marshall, the Mayor of Colyford, dressed to officiate at the Michaelmas Goose Fayre, 1990. The Borough of Colyford was founded in 1225 by Thomas Bassett and although the position of mayor is now only ceremonial, the mayor and burgesses are still the hub of the modern village. (Express & Echo)

4

The Seaside

Making sandcastles on the beach is an absorbing game for children on holiday, and here in Exmouth during April 1991 two girls have completed a circle of sandcastles and decorated the centre with seashells. The millions of tiny grains of sand that make up the long shore at Exmouth are the product of erosion by the weathering of sandstone – together they enable people to indulge in the age-old pastime of building sandcastles. Judging by the clothes these girls are wearing, it must have been a cold day, but you see by their happy smiles that they were certainly enjoying themselves. (Express & Echo)

Seaton beach, August 1965. During the summer months motor-boat trips around the bay were very popular with visitors. The local fishermen were always ready to give their experience and assistance, and fishing for mackerel, pollock and whiting was always available, with the boat owners providing the lines and bait. E168, *Anita*, with local fisherman Eddie Snell in charge, is seen picking up passengers for a fishing trip. (Express & Echo)

After the First World War, the first visitors to the East Devon seaside resorts began to appear, and here on Beer beach during the summer of 1923 two young ladies enjoy the sun. The low-slung canvas and wooden deckchairs pictured here were essential for anyone who wanted to relax on the beach in comfort. The girl on the right was a charming young woman, her smile like a golden beam of light, the sun seeming to rest on her. (*Seaton Museum*)

Seaton fishermen, 1925. Before the 1920s, Seaton fishermen caught mackerel and herring in shoals. They kept three large boats, which were each rowed by four men, with a huge net in each boat. The nets were pulled onto the beach with the catches of thousands of fish. Mr G. Mutter, the fishmonger, purchased the fish and they were sent in boxes, via Seaton station, to large towns. However, by 1925 the local fishing industry was already failing, partly due to the sudden disappearance of the herring, the main source of income in the winter. In this photograph members of the well-known local fishing families of Newton and Wilkins are seen. The patriarch of the Wilkins family, known as Gentleman Jim Wilkins, is pictured here at the rear, standing against the boat. (*Ted Gosling Collection*)

The pleasure steamer the *Duchess of Devonshire* conveyed passengers to Bournemouth and Weymouth from Torquay, calling on its way at Sidmouth, Seaton and Lyme Regis. Although these towns had no pier, passengers got ashore via a small bridge thrown out to the beach from the boat. In 1934 the *Duchess* was wrecked at Sidmouth, having got into difficulties because of a heavy swell and came in on Sidmouth beach broadside. All the passengers were taken off safely, but the old steamer, pictured here a wreck on Sidmouth beach, was dismantled where she lay. (Express & Echo)

This attractive young girl was a visitor to Beer during the summer of 1922. (*Seaton Museum*)

Exmouth, August 1961. On that summer's day forty years ago the generation that was to exhibit different attitudes in fashion, behaviour and thought were still children, like these enjoying a day out with their parents at this Exmouth boating pond. A way of life was coming to an end, and although the photographer did not know it, he had captured a scene of innocence soon to disappear in the 1960s. (Express & Echo)

A summer day in Exmouth, August 1979. What a way to spend a holiday! This scene of torrential rain on the seafront at Exmouth is a reminder that weather during the holiday season is not always clement. (Express & Echo)

An evocative picture from the 1960s showing a crowded beach scene at Jacobs Ladder, Sidmouth. Note the old clock tower building on the cliff. The addition in recent years of a café there and the completion in 1999 of the Clifton Walkway, which resulted in a continuous footway from the Esplanade to Jacobs Ladder beach, have proved to be popular decisions. (Express & Echo)

Lionel and Garnet Miller, two Beer fishermen, standing beside a capstan on Beer beach, 1938. Although Brixham held its position as the leading fishing port in the country until recent times, the old saying in Beer was 'Beer made Brixham and Brixham made the North Sea'. This was quite true, for the first fishermen to trawl from Brixham were men of Beer in their small boats. The best weather for trawling was a stiff breeze of not less than force 6, but this made the old Beer luggers weather-bound on the beach because Beer had no harbour. As a result, Brixham, with its harbour, became the mother of trawling. Despite this, Beer is still a fishing village and the fishermen of Beer fully deserve their reputation of unsurpassed seamanship. (*Ted Gosling Collection*)

Come on in, the water is freezing. It was cold, very cold, because these people at Exmouth were not enjoying a dip in mid-summer as the rest of us would – they were some of the participants in the Christmas Day swim from Exmouth beach in 1979. (Express & Echo)

Landslip Cottage, *c.* 1890. The landslip after which this house was named occurred on Christmas Eve 1839, a mile from Rousdon. The cottagers who dwelt on the borders of the cliffs were alarmed by a strange and unaccountable noise, resembling the rumbling of thunder. Noticing that the walls of their homes were cracking and sinking, they made good their escape. During all of Christmas Day the whole place began to drop gently, but with a dreadful persistence, until three-quarters of a mile of cultivated land had crashed down upon the undercliff, carrying with it 45 acres of arable land, two cottages and an orchard. The cottage seen here provided refreshments for visitors to the landslip. It is said to have been built from the materials of one of the two cottages that were damaged in the slip. The cottage has now gone, but members of the older generation still recall with delight the walk to the landslip and the splendid cream teas and the old-fashioned hospitality shown by the Gapper family who lived at Landslip Cottage. (*Seaton Museum*)

Ladram Bay, photographed by Francis Bedford, *c.* 1855. Here the sea has carved the cliffs into spectacular shapes and isolated blocks of sandstone from the mainland at Ladram Bay, near Otterton. (*Ted Gosling Collection*)

Seaton's nightmare began before daybreak on Tuesday morning, 13 February 1979 when strong winds in the South Western approaches combined with a heavy groundswell to create an abnormally high tide which advanced across the beach and smashed into the seafront homes and hotels. The weather conditions that eventually caused the damage at Seaton had built up several days earlier, some 1,500 nautical miles away in the mid-North Atlantic. A depression from this area moved at such speed that it generated high waves of unusually long periods and large wave lengths. These waves swept into the English Channel and coincided with a series of spring tides. A total of 43 homes and 28 business premises were damaged, together with 240 self-catering chalets and 250 dormer chalets at the two holiday camps. Following this flooding, a new £600,000 sea wall and promenade was built at the resort by South West Water. The photograph above shows the seafront at Seaton just after the incident, with the aftermath of the flooding. In the photograph below, taken on 28 February 1980, work is being carried out on the new sea wall. (*Seaton Museum*)

Fishing is still a way of life in Beer, and the fishermen of this village are among the most skilful sailors to be found in Britain. At the beginning of the twentieth century Beer beach was a very busy place, with fishing boats packed from one end to the other. Today, catering for tourism plays a far more important role in the village. In the photograph above, Beer beach is seen during early summer, *c.* 1980. The photograph below was taken after a storm in the 1970s. (*Ted Gosling Collection*)

A high tide and adverse weather conditions swept a varied assortment of jetsam over Exmouth beach on 18 March 1987. The young volunteers of the beach patrol are seen here helping out with the big tidy up. (Express & Echo)

The collapsed section of Exmouth pier, which was caused by bad weather conditions during February 1984. (Express & Echo)

Sidmouth beach, 1895. Following a time-honoured right, all the families of Sidmouth fishermen had their own sections of the beach to work. The bathing machines by the seashore in the foreground of the photograph belonged to the Woolley family. These contraptions had two compartments, one for disrobing and a 'wet' section for putting on the costumes. It was pushed down to the sea until the wheels were half submerged, ladies then went down three steps to stand in the sea. These bathing machines were a familiar sight on the beaches of the East Devon seaside resorts until the beginning of the twentieth century. (*Ted Gosling Collection*)

The wreck of the *Berar*, October 1896. This three-masted Italian barque was on her way from Finland to Spain laden with about 1,200 tons of planks when she ran into difficulties. In tacking from Casquets, off the coast of France, to Start Point in the face of strong westerly gales, the captain unsuccessfully attempted to make for Portland. Thick weather came on and the gales increased in force, so that the vessel could only be sailed under close-reefed topsails and staysails. The captain then lost his bearings and the force of the wind and waves drove her broadside on the rocks near Rousdon. The crew, which consisted of Captain Bertolotto, thirteen men and two boys, nearly all of Italian nationality, managed to reach dry land in safety. (*Ted Gosling Collection*)

Major seaside resorts mix with the peace and quiet of the East Devon countryside, making the area a favourite spot for holiday-makers. The beaches and surrounding area are obvious places for the swimming, boating and walking enthusiasts, but the sporting attractions of the area are many and varied and appeal to almost every taste. Many visitors to East Devon prefer the freedom of a holiday park, where they can book a luxury caravan and enjoy the recreational facilities that are available. In the photograph above, Sandy Bay Holiday Park is seen, near the village of Littleham, July 1985. In the photograph below, taken at the same time, is Lyme Bay Holiday Park in Seaton. (Express & Echo)

The Sea Shanty at Branscombe Mouth, 1970s. In the nineteenth century a building at Branscombe Mouth was used to store the 'culm' brought by sea from South Wales to fuel the lime kilns on the cliffs. This old building was transformed into a thatched tea room, known as The Sea Shanty, and is now visited by thousands of tourists. The three ladies appear to be enjoying themselves – after all is said and done, it would be a hard job to find a better place for a picnic and a spot of knitting. (Express & Echo)

Exmouth, 27 August 1969. A seaside holiday in East Devon is still essentially a family one. Although the weather can be unreliable, you can see in this photograph that the children on the swing-boats are really enjoying a day out. (Express & Echo)

The Parade and beach at Exmouth, *c.* 1908. By the Edwardian period seaside holidays had become very popular, especially for day-trippers. At Exmouth and other resorts there were many delights to please young and old alike. In this photograph there are still some of those ancient bathing machines which were fast being replaced by rows of painted wooden changing huts. The beach looks very quiet, and two men are painting a gas-lamp standard, so it is probably early in the summer season. (*Ted Gosling Collection*)

The Parade and beach, looking east, Sidmouth, 1937. I have always thought that the 1930s were depressing years which seem to carry a feeling of autumn about them. Certainly it was a middle-class decade, which in East Devon was most obvious in Sidmouth, and this is well reflected in this beach scene. (*S. Luxton*)

Holiday-makers are well catered for at The World of Country Life at Sandy Bay, near Exmouth. Children can mingle with the lambs, rabbits and chickens in the pets centre and enjoy meeting the resident donkeys. The family can wander down a Victorian street and enjoy the quiet life in the Keepers Cottage. A section is devoted to the transport and agricultural machinery of the past, and a vast collection of vintage cars brings back memories of vehicles our grandparents drove. In the photograph above, Sarah and Matthew Backwell are feeding the young lambs in the pets corner during June 1989. In the photograph below, two young girls admire an Austin 7 sports car. (Express & Echo)

A walk on the wild side – two visitors go for a stroll on the beach at Exmouth, July 1988. To most people a shingle beach is an immovable object that hurts bare feet, but the shingle is always shifting, especially between high and low tides and its movement is complex. (Express & Echo)

The Hotel Riviera, Sidmouth, with guests and a fine Edwardian motor car outside, *c.* 1910. The unspoilt beauty of the surrounding countryside, the excellent hotels and shops and the mild climate have always attracted the more discriminating visitor to Sidmouth, and in the 1960s only six towns or cities had a greater number of hotels. The Hotel Riviera was a terrace of three-storey houses that were built in 1820, and which were later converted to a hotel. Today the hotel, with its fine position in the centre of the Esplanade, is noted for excellent food and comfort. (*Norman Lambert*)

5

In & Around the Country

Hay-making in Vicarage Field, Seaton, *c.* 1905. The workers seen here are, left to right: Messrs Long, Newton, Pearce, Real, Peach, Sellars and Chant. The little boy in the photograph was a member of the Peach family. Although by this time the mechanical reaper did most of the work on the farm, Vicarage Field was small and it was not worth bringing in a mowing machine to do the job. The present-day Case Gardens were built on Vicarage Field. (*Ted Gosling Collection*)

The Stoke Hill Foot Beagles and supporters gather in Seaton cricket field to hunt hares in the marshes, 6 November 1912. It has been said that although the hare has the maximum number of enemies it is singularly equipped to elude them. It is long-sighted, has quick ears and a keen sense of smell. It is also capable of a clean jump of 3 to 4 yd from its resting place. Hares live in well-defined territories, and before the First World War were common in the Seaton marshes. In this more enlightened age they are no longer hunted by packs of dogs, but our forefathers had different values. (*Ted Gosling Collection*)

A traction engine that was used on the estate of W.H. Head Esq., *c.* 1901. The belt driven by the traction engine worked a large circular saw, which cut the blocks of wood on the roller bench into planks. W.H. Head, of The Wessiters, Seaton, is standing on the extreme left with friends and workers. This photograph illustrates well how the English countryside became mechanised towards the end of the nineteenth century. (*Ted Gosling Collection*)

Mary Broom's working farmhouse kitchen fireplace, *c.* 1959. Mary Broom farmed in Axmouth, and above her mantelpiece is a rack for the long spits used over wood fires. The floor has its original paving of irregularly shaped pieces of flat stone and, although not seen in this photograph, I expect that somewhere was hanging a brass and copper warming pan. In the East Devon farmhouse the principal room was the kitchen, the main features of which were the stone-flagged floor and the capacious fireplace with a cosy inglenook. In the past, unmarried farm labourers lived and boarded at the farm, so the kitchen table, made of oak, was of a size sufficient to seat over a dozen people. Standing against the wall would be huge oak dressers, which would be used to display an assortment of china on their shelves, along with dishes, platters and bowls. Working farmhouse kitchens were the centre of all household activities, and it is rare to find an unspoilt example today. (*Ted Gosling Collection*)

Hay-making near Beer, June 1932. Gathering and storing hay was obviously an important job for East Devon farmers and, although photographs like this make it appear attractive, the traditional method of hay-making was very laborious. It had to be cut with a horse-drawn mower, then picked by hand with pitchforks and loaded onto wagons to be taken back to the farm to be made into hay-ricks. The work was very hard, yet those seen here look happy. Their good humour was probably helped by the plentiful supply of cider that was made available during the break periods. In the photograph above, farm workers have just loaded the wagon. In the photograph below, Ken Tonge from Beer gives one of the cart horses a tit-bit; note the hay rake on the left. (*Seaton Museum*)

Hay-making is another important date in the East Devon farmer's calendar and the farmer at Hayne Farm in Awliscombe managed to get soldiers from the Heathfield Camp at Honiton to help him in 1957. Hay provides much of the winter feed for farming stock, so getting the hay cut and dried takes top priority and all help in getting it stacked is gratefully received. The grass for hay is usually ready for mowing in June or July, and we all know that storms with heavy rain can occur during the summer months. The soldiers seen here are sitting on a farm wagon and the man in the centre is holding young David Joslin on his lap. (*Joslin*)

Friesian cows peacefully chewing the cud beside a quiet river near Whitford reflect the tranquillity of life in the East Devon countryside, *c.* 1962. The Friesian, a foreigner to Devon, is a breed that was developed in the Netherlands and it is such an efficient milk producer that its introduction has nearly destroyed our native dairy breeds. Before milking parlours were installed, dairy farming was more labour intensive. We all have a false image of a happy milk-maid sitting on a stool hand-milking the cows, but in reality it was a dirty job, and it took two men all their time to hand-milk thirty-five cows. It was also hard work, especially during the cold weather, when you had to fetch them in from muddy fields. (*Ted Gosling Collection*)

Rabbit catching near Luppitt, *c.* 1890. In those pre-myxomatosis days a good catch could be made with a couple of ferrets. A net was arranged around the warren and ferrets put into the holes to drive out the rabbits, which were then either shot or trapped in the net. These men worked on a local estate, but many farm hands used rabbit catching to supplement their income. (*Ted Gosling Collection*)

A welcome break for tea during hay-making at Couchill Farm, near Beer, 1930s. Left to right: Mr Thomas, Ernest Wilson, Mr Thomas Sr, Mr Carslake and another Mr Thomas. Mr Thomas Sr was the father of the other two Thomases. (*Seaton Museum*)

Devon is famous for its cider, and this old song gives a guarantee of long life to those who drink it:

In an East Devon village not far from the sea
Still lives my old Gran-dad aged ninety and three
Of orchards and meadows he owns a good lot
Such as his – not another has got.
My Gran-dad is lusty, is nimble and spry
As Ribstons his cheeks, clear as crystal his eye,
His head snowy white as the flowering May
And he drinks only cider by night and by day.

Cider presses were commonplace at the turn of the last century, when nearly every farm in East Devon made its own cider. Nowadays cider presses are antiques much coveted by in-comers to give a period flavour to their restored country cottages. Sad to think that they have lapsed from common use to become valued merely as decorations. Devon is a county with near-perfect conditions for apple growing and the firm Green Valley Cyder, which operate from Darts Farm Shopping Village of Clyst St George, is dedicated to continuing and developing the best traditions of cider-making in the county. Green Valley cider has even been on the menu at the House of Commons. In the photograph above, the owner of Green Valley Cyder Chris Coles is seen taking a sample of the juice from the press. In the photograph below, Hugh Vincent and Larry Pope are levelling the apple pulp during cheese building – the squeezed pulp is termed the 'cheese'. (*By permission Green Valley Cyder; copyright Nigel Albright*)

In the towns and villages of East Devon the churches, with their towers that dominate the skyline, are often the oldest surviving buildings. It was during the twelfth century that a vast building programme of churches, both large and small, took place, and from that time they became the centre of communal life, giving spiritual comfort to those in need. The sixteenth century saw the introduction of parish registers to record births, baptisms, marriages and deaths in the community. These registers, together with the plaques and tombstones, give a social history of the village. In the photograph above, the Church of St Michael at Axmouth is seen in 1958. Parts of the present structure date from the twelfth century. In the photograph below, the Church of St Mary at Luppitt is seen in 1935. This church is a fourteenth-century cruciform building. (*Ted Gosling Collection*)

Result of a shoot near Branscombe, *c.* 1905. The man sitting on the far left is W.H. Head Esq. from Seaton, but little is known about the other people. The man standing on the left and the man sitting on the far right were almost certainly beaters. The four guns were well dressed by today's standards and were definitely not local farmers. I should imagine taking high birds could have proved uncomfortable for the man wearing the high-collar shirt, but in the Edwardian period dress standards had to be maintained. (*Seaton Museum*)

Although the first motor cars made their appearance in East Devon at the beginning of the twentieth century, the horse was still supreme at this time. The horse gave employment to a large number of people in East Devon, from wheelwrights, blacksmiths, saddlers and harness-makers to stablemen, grooms and coachmen. Some of those workers are seen here. In the photograph above, John Gosling, who worked as a gardener and groom at Halsdon House, near Luppitt, stands in the middle of the group, *c.* 1898. The other two people are unknown, but it is quite apparent from her attire that the young lady on his left did not belong to the domestic staff of the house. (*Ted Gosling Collection*)

An early spring morning in 1930 and these visitors to East Devon have stopped their car near Blackbury Castle for a picnic. It must have been one of those days you get in February and March, with patches of blue sky and gleams of sun, but you can see by the way they are wrapped up that it was still cold. The lady on the left, smoking a cigarette, is holding what appears to be an empty whisky bottle and, by the look on her face, she was adding more than a nip to keep the chill out. (*Ted Gosling Collection*)

Dr Tonge from Beer, wearing his trilby hat, is pictured skating arm-in-arm with a friend, who appears to be warmly dressed for the occasion, 1929. During the early months of this year East Devon suffered an intense frost and the ice on Bovey Pond, near Beer, became thick enough to allow skating. Many people came out to the pond to enjoy the fun, and when it grew dark the area was lit with lanterns and people skated with torches. (*Seaton Museum*)

The coming of the railway contributed much to the development of East Devon's seaside towns, and for countless generations of holiday-makers Axminster was the gateway to their final destination. The Southern Railway travelled via Axminster and Honiton, with branch lines pushing down to the seaside resorts of Seaton, Sidmouth, Budleigh Salterton and Exmouth. The railway network in Devon was to remain virtually intact until the re-shaping of the British railways in the Beeching Report of 1963, which advocated closure for most of the branch lines throughout the country. The result was a disaster for East Devon. The photograph above shows Sidmouth Junction, looking west towards Whimple, *c.* 1955. The junction stood in the village of Feniton and was still a busy place in 1955. The photograph below shows Seaton Junction, looking west towards Honiton Banks, with a S.15 class on an Up stopping train, *c.* 1958. (*Mike Clement Collection*)

Campanology – most people are delighted when they hear a peal of bells from their local church on a Sunday morning, and possibly on a practice night during the week. Learning to ring bells is exceedingly difficult, with many complicated and technical elements. In the photograph above, taken on 15 August 1937, are the Seaton Ringers. Back row, left to right: F.R. Browett, F. Abbott, A.H. Bradford; middle row: A. Gigg, T.O. Hilder; front row: J. Board, W. Boundy (captain), G. Northcott. In the photograph below are the ringers from Awliscombe, *c.* 1955. Left to right: John Lemon, John Summers, Mrs Philips, Bob Summers, George Dyer, Ben Baker, Jim Wheaton, Derek Dimond, John Underdown, Dick Summers. (*Above: Seaton Museum; below: Joslin*)

Shute, 1962. The gate-house of Shute Barton dominates the village, inviting the passing visitor to go through the narrow entrance to explore a world of manorial splendour. The house was partly demolished in 1787, but much early work remains, including the fireplace, which is said to be one of the broadest in Europe. The great medieval lords of Shute were the Bonvilles, the powerful antagonists of the Courtenays during the fifteenth century. It then came to the Petres, who sold it to Sir John Pole Bt. in 1787. It was Sir John who knocked down some of Shute Barton and constructed Shute House between 1787 and 1790. This building, with its fine rooms, was in recent years converted to luxury flats and Shute Barton, one of the most important surviving non-fortified manor houses of the Middle Ages, now belongs to the National Trust. (*Ted Gosling Collection*)

Members of the Axe Valley Heritage Association are seen gathered around Norman Whinfrey, who was giving a talk on Blackbury Castle when the association paid a visit to the site in 1987. The enclosure is of Iron Age date, not later than 200 BC. It is roughly oval, or perhaps a D-shape, with the bowed side to the south, on which there is the only original entrance, roughly central. It is defended by a single bank and ditch. It should not really be called a 'castle', since this is misleading and, in any event, 'bury' means the strong or fortified place. (*Ted Gosling Collection*)

The Honiton Christmas Poultry Show at Mackarness Hall, Honiton, *c.* 1957. At the front of the hall are Jack Luxton, Pat Leisk and John Stoodley, staff members of auctioneers T. Hussey and Son, who were conducting the show. People in the crowd include Harry Aggar, Dolly Lowman, Ada Pollard, Win Rattenbury, Gertie Swift, Mrs Atkins, Ernie Baker, Marie Moore and Frank Loud. (*John Stoodley*)

Opening the new auction ring at Honiton Market is Richard Marker, president of the Honiton and District Christmas Fat Stock Show, with auctioneers A.G. Luxton and Andrew and Keith Luxton, December 1990. (Express & Echo)

Lyn Bagwell, Branscombe's blacksmith, shaping a red-hot bar into a shoe on the anvil, *c.* 1988. The blacksmith still plays a vital part in village life, carrying out metal work of any kind. A modern smith is not only capable of on-the-spot repairs, but will also work as a farrier. In the small East Devon village of Branscombe times have changed – a woman has entered into what was traditionally a man's world. Nowadays most shoeing is done cold, although a better fit is obtained with a hot shoe, cooled slightly in water before being nailed on. (Express & Echo)

Feeding the poultry at Halsdon House, near Luppitt, *c.* 1885. The unhurried pace of life in Victorian England is successfully preserved in this carefully composed photograph of the out-door staff at Halsdon House. In the East Devon countryside in those days not only ordinary working households kept poultry, but the 'big house' would ensure they had their own supply of fresh eggs. This was long before the age of chickens kept in batteries as food-producing machines, they were then free to roam and enjoy a more contented life, producing a far more tasty egg. (*Ted Gosling Collection*)

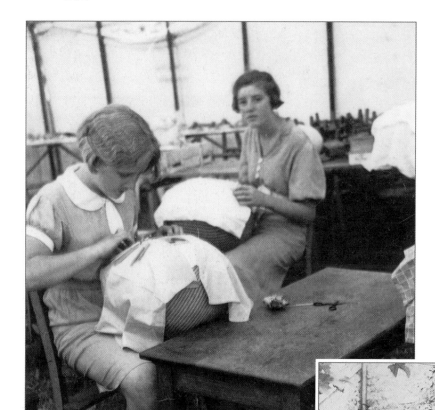

In the nineteenth century, lace-making was a cottage
industry in East Devon, which enabled women to
supplement the incomes of their farming and fishing
husbands. Lace would be taken to a local dealer, and
many of these operated a 'truck' system, taking the
lace in exchange for food. Sir Walter Trevelyan's wife
Pauline thought this most unfair, and endeavoured to
put an end to the practice. Even when paid with
money, the lace-makers worked for a pitiful wage. It
was the dealers who made the profit, and most of them
lived in Honiton. The best lace in Devon came from
Beer and, in 1840, villager Jane Bidney was
commissioned to make the bridal dress for the young
Queen Victoria. She employed a hundred of the best
lace-makers in East Devon to help her create the dress,
which cost £1,000 – at that time this must have
seemed like a fortune. The photograph above was taken
at the Beer Flower Show during August 1937 and
shows two young Beer girls busy at lace-making. In the
photograph on the right, a Beer village dame sits
outside her open cottage doorway with a lace pillow on
her lap – a scene that was common during the
nineteenth century. (*Ted Gosling Collection*)

Axe Vale Harriers, 1905. The neighbourhood of the Axe Valley was hunted by the Axe Vale Harriers, and took in country extending from Lyme to the east, to Sidmouth in the west, and from Honiton and Axminster to the north, to the sea. At the time of this photograph, earths were very numerous, owing chiefly to the fact that there were a large number of badgers in the district. The hounds were established by Mr John Dashwood Lang of Sidbury in 1880, drafts being obtained from Mr Pynsent Matthew of Rydon House and Mr Churchill Langdon, then master of the Seavington Harriers. The kennels were then at Harcombe near Sidmouth. In 1885 Mr Lang gave up the pack and the kennels were removed to Seaton. The pack consisted of sixteen couples of hounds of the old badger-pye colour, with a standard of about 21 in. Seen here are the master Mr J. Impey-Scarbrough, second from the left, and the huntsman Mr W.H. Head, on the right. (*Seaton Museum*)

East Devon has a rich array of wildlife habitats, from the high heaths and grasslands of the Blackdown Hills through to the lowlands with their ancient woods rich in birds and flowers. The county is home to the internationally famous Exe estuary and the unique Pebblebed Heaths with their nightjars and Dartford warblers. By far the greatest portion of the district consists of rich farming land, much of which remains valuable for wildlife, especially where old hedgerows and unimproved grasslands have survived. East Devon is a part of the country where hearts beat at a different pace, a place where true Devonians know not only where their food comes from but that small farmers still care more for the land than anyone else. Unfortunately, this could all change in the future as large scale agribusinesses, aiming more at the export market, become the order of the day. In the photograph on the left is a hare with his large ears alert. In the photograph below is a little egret, *egretta garzetta*, which has over-wintered on the Axe estuary. (*Left: Devon Wildlife Trust; below: Axe Vale Conservation Society*)

6

The Children

May Day celebrations in the playground of Awliscombe Village School, 1967. The month of May is dedicated to the Virgin Mary and is symbolised by the crowning of the Queen of the May on May Day. Some village schools still celebrate the custom and once, not so long ago, to be May Queen was the dream of many a little girl. The May Queen can be seen seated on the right, and the children are dancing under the keen eye of a teacher. (*Joslin*)

All Saints School, Sidmouth, c. 1855. The school was built in 1847 and enlarged in 1904 to accommodate an additional sixty pupils. This image, one of the earliest in this book, was produced by the collodion or wet-plate process. Introduced in 1851, this method was used almost exclusively for photographs until the 1870s. Clearly in those far-off days a group photograph was something exciting, and the process itself considered to be somewhat miraculous. The photographer must have been a most accomplished artist, and the natural restlessness of children, especially as they must have been facing a camera for the first time in their lives, did not prevent him from obtaining this excellent picture. (*Ted Gosling Collection*)

The children of Luppitt School celebrating the coronation of Edward VII, 1902. The pupils were assembled by headmaster George Berry, seen standing to the left, to have this photograph taken by Mr W.E. Berry, the Luppitt photographer. He recorded a scene of great charm, depicting a quaint, old-fashioned group, the girls in their ankle-length frocks and white pinafores and the boys in hobnail boots. It must have been a memorable day for the children, whose lives were restricted by poverty and other hardships. Occasions like this were an escape from the narrow world in which they lived. (*Ted Gosling Collection*)

Sir Walter Trevelyan School, Seaton, 1907. Jenks White, a teacher who taught at the school for over forty years, is standing on the right, and next to him is Miss Tozer, who remained at the school until her retirement in 1949. Headmaster Mr Oldridge can be seen on the left of the picture. (*Seaton Museum*)

Woodroffe School Early Music Group entertain at the Colyford Goose Fayre, September 1991. (Express & Echo)

Malvern House School for Girls was evacuated from Lewisham during the Second World War and was housed in the Manor House at Seaton. It was at this time that the name was changed to the Manor House School. Following many years of mixed fortunes, which included a move to Lynwood, a house situated between Seaton and Beer, a board of governors was elected in 1958, with the Revd N. George, vicar of Seaton, as chairman. Francis and Mary Eyles were asked to take over the school, which meant that Mr Eyles had to give up his headship of Beer Primary School, and Mrs Eyles the infants class which she operated from her home in Beer. They agreed to purchase the school, and from that moment the number on the roll increased steadily, the Department of Education and Science recognising the efficiency of the school in 1965. By the summer of 1969 the school was too full, so a move was made in September 1969 to Springfield House, Honiton. It was on 1 October 1969 that the new Manor House School opened, with ninety-nine pupils. Since that date the school has grown and the high standard of education offered at the school is due totally to the members of staff. In the photograph above, the pupils and staff assemble during the spring of 1950. In the photograph below, Holly Ford from Honiton is congratulated by her father after competing at the school sports day, 1998. (*Above: Seaton Museum; below: H. Ford*)

Colyton Grammar School was founded in 1546 at a time when Henry VIII, overgrown with corpulency, was an old man waiting for death. The Speaker of the House of Commons reported that during his reign the country was poorer by 100 grammar schools. Devon, at least, was immeasurably richer by one. Since that date the school has had four homes, known all our Prime Ministers, but was only ever visited by one of them when John Major visited the school in November 1993. In the photograph above, John Major is shaking hands with the headgirl Marie Coles, to her right is headboy Michael Cole, on her left is the headmaster Mr B. Sindall and next to him is Mr David Meikle MBE, who was then chairman of governors. In the background East Devon MP Peter Emery is talking to a John Major 'minder'. In the photograph below, John Major, with Mike Cummings, head of technology, talks to students Adam Wallis on his left and Gary Harper on his right. (Express & Echo)

Pupils from Ottery St Mary County Primary School during a trip to Exeter Airport, hosted by Jersey European Airways, January 1993. The schoolchildren, who were doing a project on flying, split into two groups for their tour of the airport. During their visit a question and answer session was given by one of the airline's senior pilots, Ted Nance. (Express & Echo)

All schools are now equipped with PCs, and when French students visited Kings School, Ottery St Mary, during November 1991 they were photographed sharing computer time with the pupils. In today's high-tech world computers play an ever-increasing role and tasks that would once have taken hours can be accomplished in minutes. (Express & Echo)

Pupils at Colyton Grammar School got a taste of the high life when they sampled rock climbing with army experts, *c.* 1993. Members of the Devon and Dorset Regiment's youth display team are pictured here with their giant climbing wall and aerial slide. (Express & Echo)

Honiton Primary School pupils taking part in a mock wedding, March 1991. Front row, left to right: Nicola Monk, Matthew Mustafic, Joel Pridmore, Katie Spiller, Zoe McLachlan, Shaun Hughes; back row: Kelly Palmer, Gemma Clancy, Nicola Burroughs. (Express & Echo)

Children taking part in the Nativity play *One Night in Bethlehem* at Awliscombe parish church, December 1962. The cast featured the following young people, many of whom are seen here: Mary – Helen Furnival, Joseph – Francis Pring, innkeeper – Nigel Pouleen, innkeeper's wife – Pauline Manley, Sarah – Marian Hounsell, shepherds – Roland Housell, Malcolm Davey, Graham Braddick, David Joslin, Christopher Manley, David Hill and the Kings – Michael Marks, Michael Hill and Kenneth Gush. (*Joslin*)

Opposite, above: The pleasure that an old custom has given to generations of locals is reflected on the faces of these children, Good Friday 1988. The distribution of hot cross buns on the Bedford Lawn, Sidmouth, was introduced in 1898. The bakers of Sidmouth had decided against making buns on Good Friday, but a member of the council, Mr J.P. Millen, and other townsmen subscribed and got Mr Wheaton, a baker from Newton Poppleford, to supply 2,000 buns for all the children in Sidmouth. The buns were to be given away on Good Friday, between 8 a.m. and 9 a.m., on Bedford Lawns. Following the death of Mr Millen the custom was taken up by the local lodge of RAOB and continues to the present day. (Express & Echo)

Opposite, below: Residents in Charles Road, Honiton, are seen here in March 1985 protesting against East Devon District Council's decision to erect a 5-ft concrete post and wire mesh fence around the children's play area without asking them. Three swings stood on a grassed area in the middle of the cul-de-sac and the children used to play cricket there. This came to an end because the fencing split the ground into three sections. (Express & Echo)

The earliest record of Honiton Fair is in 1221, when it took place on All-Hallows Day, 1 November. The date of the fair was changed in 1247 to the eve and feast of St Margaret, 19/20 July, and it still takes place at this time. The fair is opened by an event known as the glove ceremony, when the town crier, in his robes, appears bearing a pole decorated with flowers and surmounted by a large stuffed glove, painted gold. He then announces the opening of the fair with these words: 'Oyez, oyez, oyez. The glove is up, the glove is up, the glove is up.' After this follows another custom of unknown origin, the throwing of the hot pennies. The photograph above was taken on 23 July 1991, and here youngsters are pocketing the pennies thrown to them from the first-floor window of a pub. In the photograph below, dated 21 July 1992, fourteen-year-old Alex Carter is seen showering the crowd from a convenient balcony, surely a case of 'pennies from heaven'. (Express & Echo)

On 8 May 1945 the war in Europe ended, and a two-day national holiday was declared. Free entertainment, communal lunches and tea parties were staged in the streets. In Britain's customary way of signalling victory, since the time of the Armada, massive bonfires were lit on prominent sites and a tremendous feeling of relief spread over the whole of East Devon. Fifty years on, and the nation felt it was again time to commemorate VE Day, and once more people responded in a magnificent way. Church services took place, followed by children's sports and street tea parties. The day was blessed with good weather, and everyone made sure that the younger generation were reminded of what was being celebrated. In the photograph above, children are enjoying a tea party in the High Street, Colyton, 8 May 1995. In the photograph below, taken on the same day, the children of Beer are also having a good time. (*John Lavers/Seaton Museum*)

Margaret Rogers, chairman of Devon County Council Scrutiny Committee for Education and Social Services, making a presentation to Jamie Courtney and Dean Barden at the Offwell Primary School leavers service in the village hall, July 2001. The pupils are receiving a coveted Certificate of Excellence, awarded by the Department of Education to schools attaining high Key Stage 2 results. The award was for the year 1999–2000, when it was first introduced by the Government, but did not arrive at the school until a few weeks before this event. Headteacher Helen Teare said, 'naturally we are delighted at gaining the award, it was the result of a team effort by all our staff'. Devon Education Committee vetted applications for the certificate and the Government chose the national finalists. The cash prize issued with the certificate was shared among staff, and was based on the size of the school. Offwell, which now has ninety-five pupils, was awarded £1,600. (*Colin Bowerman*)

7

High Days & Events

Royal Glen Hotel, 1887. This splendid four-in-hand with a coach load of passengers must have formed some part of Queen Victoria's Golden Jubilee celebrations in 1887. Originally known as Woolbrook Cottage, the Royal Glen was built in 1809 and it was here, just before Christmas 1819, that the Duke and Duchess of Kent stayed with their seven-month-old daughter Victoria, the future Queen. While here, the young princess had a narrow escape when a boy shooting sparrows in the road outside broke a window with a bullet, which narrowly grazed the sleeve of the baby princess. (*Ted Gosling Collection*)

The Colyford Goose Fayre was resurrected in 1982 under the direction of the then Mayor of the Borough of Colyford Colin Pady, with the enthusiastic support of the burgesses and villagers. The right to hold a seven-day Michaelmas fair was originally granted to Sir Thomas Bassett by King John in 1208 and the Borough of Colyford was founded shortly after, although the Charter was not presented until 1341. In the thirteenth century, the granting of a fair was sought by major landholders as a means of increasing their income. When the decision was taken to revive the fair, it was decided to model it on a typical Michaelmas goose fair of the medieval period. The fair is now a popular and colourful local event, as can be seen from these photographs. In the photograph above, villagers and guests are dressed in medieval costume for Colyford Goose Fayre, 25 September 1993. In the photograph below is archer Brian Cooper, a member and treasurer of the Lacetown Archers from Honiton, on 26 September 1992. (Express & Echo)

The Ottery St Mary Carnival, which is held on 5 November, attracts wide interest throughout the West Country. The celebrations commence at daybreak, when the good folk of Ottery are awakened by the sound of explosions from a 'rock cannon'. The carnival procession takes place in the evening, when a large number of tableaux, headed by the carnival queen and her attendants, parade through the town. A 'guy' is also carried in the procession, escorted by bearers carrying flaming torches. This effigy of Guy Fawkes is burnt on a large bonfire in a meadow by the river at St Saviour's. The town is known worldwide for the main event of the day, 'the rolling of the tar barrels'. In the afternoon there is a boys' barrel, and in the photograph above, you can see the crowd parting at the last minute to let the boy carry the blazing tar barrel through the packed street, *c.* 1995. In the photograph below, a colourful walking group entry from the Kings School in Ottery St Mary pose for this pre-procession picture, *c.* 1995. (*Colin Bowerman*)

Pecorama is one of East Devon's leading visitor attractions, home of Peco, the world's foremost manufacturer of model railway track, and the location for the award-winning Beer Heights Light Railway. Superbly crafted layouts in many gauges of track greet visitors to the Peco railway exhibition, while outdoors the 7¼-in gauge miniature railway carries passengers on a mile-long ride through flower-filled gardens, steep-sided cuttings and a long, dark tunnel. On site the 'Orion' Pullman car gives you a glimpse into the past, to the days of luxury travel. The 'Orion', which now serves coffee, tea, cream teas and cakes, caused a stir in the village of Beer when it arrived after its long road journey from Wolverton. In the photograph above, 'Orion', in all its glory, is seen entering Mare Lane from The Causeway, a gradient of 1 in 5, on 8 February 1978. In the photograph below, the founder of Pecorama Mr Sydney Pritchard, on the left, welcomes Mr Bill McMillan from Glasgow, who opened the renovated 'Orion' Pullman coach, 15 June 1978. Making him feel at home is piper Mr John Fogarty. (Express & Echo)

Members of the Axe Vale and District Conservation Society, led by Mr P.R. Noakes OBE, get ready to travel on the Seaton Tramway to view the River Axe and its wading birds, *c.* 1990. The Seaton Tramway company originated at the Lancaster Electrical Company of Barnet, which manufactured battery electric vehicles. In 1949 the owner Claude Lane indulged his hobby by building a miniature 15-in gauge tram, which he ran at garden fêtes and community events. This portable system enjoyed temporary homes at St Leonard's (Sussex) and Rhyl (North Wales) before evolving into the 2-ft gauge Eastbourne Tramway in 1954. Many of the present trams were built at Eastbourne but by the mid-1960s the tramway's success was outgrowing the ⅔-mile line, which in any case was under threat from housing development. Claude Lane therefore began to look for alternative locations. Meanwhile, the Seaton branch railway was under threat of closure. The 4½-mile line ran from Seaton to Seaton Junction, on the Exeter–Waterloo main line. The branch was opened in 1868 by the Seaton & Beer Railway Company, primarily to transport Beer limestone. They sold out to the London & South Western Railway in 1885, which in turn became part of the Southern Railway in 1923; by this time, the main cargo was tourists. Following nationalisation in 1947, the line passed to British Railways Western Region, but car ownership was already causing a decline in passengers. The infamous Beeching Report was the last straw and the line finally closed in 1966. Claude Lane purchased the Seaton–Colyton section in late 1969 and, after a mammoth relocation from Eastbourne, the first section of the 2-ft 9-in gauge Seaton Tramway opened in August 1970. Despite Claude Lane's death in 1971, the tramway continued and the final extension to Colyton was opened in 1980. Seaton Tramway is now one of the area's leading visitor attractions, thanks to the dedication of Claude Lane's successor Allan Gardner and his fellow directors, staff and volunteers, but chiefly because of the thousands of delighted visitors who make this unique journey each year. (*Seaton Museum*)

A frustrating feature of the work of a museum curator responsible for collections of old photographs is the large number that bear neither date nor subject name. This group of Colyton men must have worked for Warren & Carnell, whose lorry can be seen in the centre of this picture. This photograph was probably taken in the 1930s and, judging by the smart attire and button holes, it could have been on the occasion of a firm's outing. Any information would be welcome. (*Seaton Museum*)

Committee members receiving unique visitors at Axminster Carnival, 1923. (*Norman Lambert*)

Seaton Hospital was officially opened on Tuesday, 10 May 1988 by HRH the Duchess of Gloucester. Having cost over £680,000, huge support from the hospital's League of Friends over the previous few years secured the town its first ever hospital, ending many long trips to Axminster and further still to Honiton and Exeter. The League, which was formed in anticipation of the hospital, raised over £70,000 for the 24-bed bungalow-style hospital, particularly for the physiotherapy unit, and in addition many trees and shrubs were donated for the gardens. The turf-cutting for the community hospital had been performed about eighteen months before by local GP Dr Bob Jones when schoolchildren let off hundreds of balloons to celebrate. Building work was completed by contractors Skinner Construction of Sidmouth earlier in the year. Designed by architects Kendall, Kingscott Partnership of Exeter, the hospital is built around three sides of a courtyard, close to the town's health centre and a sheltered housing development in Harepath Road. In the photograph above, local volunteers are seen raising funds for the proposed hospital. In the photograph below, HRH the Duchess of Gloucester is performing the opening ceremony. (*Seaton Museum*)

The comedian Jimmy Cricket was present at Pecorama, Beer, during July 1986 to name officially a
new locomotive – *Jimmy*. After he had performed the naming ceremony, Jimmy Cricket tried his hand
at the wheel. This gala day was to raise funds for Exeter to stage the 1987 British Transplant Games.
In the picture, left to right, are Mr Sydney Pritchard, managing director of Pecorama, Mr Michael
Golby, the chief surgeon in charge of transplants at the Royal Devon and Exeter Hospital at Wonford,
train driver Mr John Cawley and, of course, Jimmy Cricket in the driving seat. (Express & Echo)

The caves that provide the beautiful Beer stone, so prized by masons, have been worked by hand since Roman times. Beer stone was used by the Romans on buildings in Exeter and in the villa discovered near Seaton. It is a cream-coloured stone when freshly quarried which turns grey upon exposure. It has been used in many of Britain's most famous buildings, such as St Paul's, Westminster Abbey, Hampton Court and Winchester Cathedral. Beer stone has also been used extensively for interior work in nearly every parish church in East Devon. Working stopped at the caves over 90 years ago, and today over 20,000 visitors a year are conducted on a 1-hour tour by expert guides, who bring back to life the reality and hardship of working underground. In the photograph above, John Scott and Gladys Gray are seen with the later medieval window tracery originally in Colyton church and now in Beer Quarry Caves underground museum. In the photograph below is one of the thousands of signatures that have been etched into the walls of the quarries – five generations of Cawleys have left their mark in the caves. (Express & Echo)

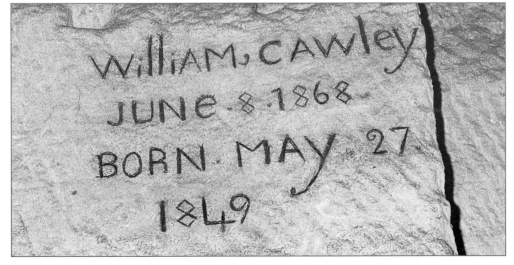

The crowning of the Branscombe Apple Pie Fayre Queen, *c.* 1952. Standing at the back on the left is Nobby Clarke, with other committee members, and in the front row is the Queen with her attendants. Front row, left to right: Maxine Pike, Sylvia Hawker, Jenny Reid and Pauline Smith. The apple is the 'fruit of fruits', and country bred men are prepared to argue that no other can compare with it. What other tree can give us the very beautiful clusters of pink and white petals that make the East Devon countryside so attractive in May, or the fruit we pick in autumn? And what about the cider, the fermented juice of the apples, once produced by local farmers from their own apples, but now a substantial factory industry? In Branscombe village the apple is celebrated by the Branscombe Apple Pie Fayre, which was revived by the Branscombe British Legion in the 1940s. The apple pies were cooked by Gerald and Stuart Collier in 2-ft squares. (*Ted Gosling Collection*)

Opposite, below: The official opening of Hawkins Racing's betting shop in New Street, Honiton, took place during December 1986. Rather than pay a celebrity to perform the opening ceremony, the firm's directors decided to make a donation of £200 to a local organisation, and Millwater School was chosen as the recipient. Hawkins Racing's director Mr Ralph Norman is pictured presenting the cheque to the Mayor of Honiton Mr Walt Summers. Also seen are directors Mrs Sue Norman and Mr Philip Smith, with the headmaster of Millwater School Mr George Hopkins standing on the right. (Express & Echo)

A display of pumpkins at Beer Social Club, 25 September 1993. We all know that pumpkins are much-loved by children, who make ghostly faces with them on Hallowe'en night (31 October). Not so many of us are familiar with the trailing plant with its heart-shaped, five-lobed leaves which produces the large, globular fruit with its edible layer next to the rind. However, the men of Beer certainly know their pumpkins, and every year in the Beer Social Club they hold a pumpkin show to find the biggest one. The pumpkin growers seen here are, left to right: Ken Westlake, John Ward and Stephen Ward. (Express & Echo)

The opening ceremony of the Mariners Hall, Beer, Saturday, 13 September 1958. Arthur Edward Good gave the Mariners Hall to the village of Beer with the thought that it would serve as a memorial to the considerable number of Master Mariners that the village had produced, as well as to those inhabitants who had made 'the calling of the sea' their livelihood. Arthur Good was a Master Mariner, one of over 140 men from Beer who achieved this rank. Pictured here outside the Mariners Hall following the ceremony are, left to right: the Revd W.H. Dormer, vicar of Beer, Percy Westlake MM, chairman of Beer Parish Council, Arthur Edward Good MM, Mrs Good and Derek Oliver Good, chairman of the management committee. (Express & Echo)

Opposite, below: Derek Gould and Sandra Moore, from Sidmouth, are standing beside a splendid 1928 Bentley, 1958. They had travelled from Sidmouth with Ted Gosling to attend the opening ceremony of the National Motor Museum, which was founded by Lord Montagu. The car on the right might be a Humber or a Standard; further information would be welcome. (*Ted Gosling Collection*)

Wiscombe Park Hill Climb, *c. 1958*. Wiscombe Park, between Seaton and Sidmouth, is beautifully situated, about a mile from Southleigh. The drive to the house was first used as a hill climb in the 1950s, and here Cedric Ebdon from Sidmouth, standing on the far right closest to the camera, is admiring a Bugatti, one of the competing cars. Ettore Bugatti built cars with the precision of fine watches, and these cars, with their distinctive horse-shoe radiators and tearing-calico exhaust sound, dominated motor sport in the 1920s. It is not clear what type this one is, but no doubt someone will be able to identify it. (*Ted Gosling Collection*)

During the 1950s, long before the days of the disco, bands like the Awliscombe Coronation Racketeers provided the music for dances in the village halls of East Devon. The man playing the violin was Frank Pring, and he was accompanied by Roy Manley, Derek Dimond and Keith Joslin on their accordions. On the right is Eda Wilmington playing the piano, with drummer John Summer in the background. (*Joslin*)

A wedding in Beer, *c.* 1929. An unknown photographer has successfully captured the feeling of excitement on the faces of the ladies, young and old, who were waiting for the bride to arrive at Beer parish church. The two girls standing on the steps were obviously bridesmaids and look slightly self-conscious. The expression on the face of the little boy standing in the front wearing the large hat seems to suggest he would like to be anywhere but here. The bride is unknown, but she might have been a member of Dr Tonge's family. (*Seaton Museum*)

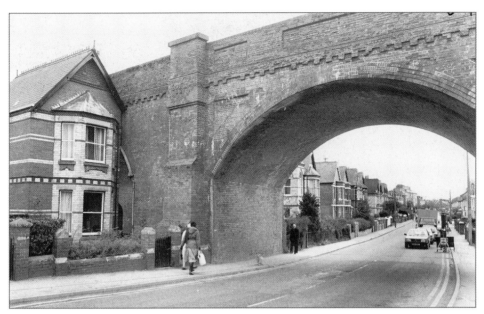

The massive brick ramparts of the Victorian bridge that once carried the Exmouth–Budleigh Salterton railway branch line is seen here just before one of the country's leading blasting demolition companies were contracted to blow it up, 1980. The bridge had to be removed without causing damage to the house, 116 Exeter Road, which stood at a distance of only 5 ft away. The job was part of the work to construct the much-needed Exmouth relief road, and the contractors Beechwood Construction Ltd were able to report that the bridge had been successfully knocked down. (Express & Echo)

Workers on Musbury village hall, *c.* 1929. Before the Second World War the village hall was the centre for social reunion and friendly competition in various games for most of the village communities in East Devon. During the late 1920s the people of Musbury were motivated to build a village hall, and this photograph shows the job near completion. (*Ted Gosling Collection*)

The colourful spectacle of carnivals is as much a part of the East Devon calendar as the seasons of sowing, harvest and Christmas. Seaton starts the ball rolling with a carnival in late August, and from that date until late November all the East Devon towns celebrate with a day of rejoicing and general gaiety. In the photograph above, Colyton Playgroup members glitter their way around the parade with their tableau 'Once upon a Rainbow' in the Colyton Carnival of September 1991. The photograph below was taken in 1957, when the Sidmouth Carnival was revived under the able chairmanship of Frank Lock. The first post-war carnival queen, seen here with her attendants, was Miss Valerie Moore, who was chosen for her outstanding, sparkling personality. (*Above: Express & Echo; below: Ted Gosling Collection*)

Some of the local Brownies and Cubs, with painted faces and dressed in brown and green pixie costumes, who raced through the town in the traditional highlight of the Ottery Pixie Day revelries, 30 June 1991. On the Saturday nearest to Midsummer Day an event known as Pixie Day has been introduced in Ottery St Mary. A number of schoolchildren take part dressed as pixies and attempt to silence the church bells by capturing the ringers. (Express & Echo)

This float was entered by J. & J.F. Baker and Co. in the Colyton Carnival in the early 1950s. The ladies seen here are, left to right: Mrs Facey, Kit Pilgrim (now Wilkes), Nina Brewer (now Filby). (*Seaton Museum*)

Operator Mrs Frances Serle, from Southleigh, welcomes Mrs Dorothea Chapple, the first passenger to use the new Beer village bus service, June 1982. This new eight-seater mini-bus ran a circular route around the village. The chairman of Devon County transport co-ordination sub-committee Mr Keith Taylor launched the service and is seen here second from left. Mr Alf Boalch, chairman of Beer Parish Council, is on his left, and Mr Roy Chapple, local councillor, is on his right. (Express & Echo)

Mr Don Potter, the secretary of the Exmouth Chamber of Trade, and his happy staff are pictured preparing to send off holiday guides from Exmouth's Tourist Information Bureau, 5 January 1988. The ladies in the photograph are, left to right: Mrs Helen Buttle, Mrs Margaret Potter, Mrs Shirley Gill. (Express & Echo)

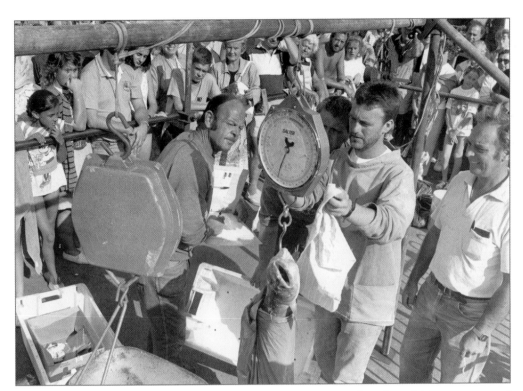

Beer people still remain the salt of the earth – their talk has not yet lost the rich Devon accent and they still retain the qualities of their forefathers. Once every year they gather together to celebrate Beer Regatta, a significant date in the diary of every Beer boy and girl. During Regatta Week the village welcomes back home the emigrants who have settled in other parts of the country, and a great gathering of the clan takes place. In the photograph above, people have congregated for the weigh-in of one of the opening events, the angling competition, showing some really fine catches, August 1989. In the photograph below, the crowds cheer on competitors in the wheel-barrow race, which took place outside the Barrel o' Beer, 10 August 1993. (Express & Echo)

The civic launch of the Honiton town bus was performed by the Mayor of Honiton Bob Walker in March 1989. The Mayor can be seen in this photograph, standing on the left beside the bus, handing out tickets to the VIPs on the inaugural run. (Express & Echo)

East Devon district councillor Mr Roy Chapple, third from left, is seen inaugurating the new town bus service at Seaton, 1 December 1981. Also taking a ride were the chairman of Seaton Town Council Mr Ted Warrington, standing in the bus next to Mr Chapple, and a number of passengers. (Express & Echo)

Sue Cannell (centre) opens the shop for the Spastics Society in Exmouth's Exeter Road, 5 April 1990. She is pictured with Area Manager Gillian Senior and Regional Administrator Lesley Ball, who were dressed as a rabbit and a duck for the occasion. Attitudes to disabled people have changed significantly in the past ten years and we no longer refer to people as 'spastic'; the correct term is now a disabled person with cerebral palsy. (Express & Echo)

Volunteers removing fairy fern from Phear Park pond, Exmouth, October 1992. *Azolla filiculoides*, commonly known as fairy fern, is a small, surface-covering aquatic plant which looks pretty innocuous when bought in garden centres to use in fish ponds. Unfortunately, when fairy fern escapes from the garden into the wild it can cause problems. The plant will grow right across lakes, ponds and even rivers, eventually blocking out all light and causing other pond and water life to die. (Express & Echo)

Every year thousands more people turn to gardening, waking up to the opportunities for transforming their outside space into a colourful garden. The people of Ottery St Mary are no exception to this and here, on 10 August 1992, television gardener Dennis Cornish presents cups to the winners of the Ottery St Mary in Bloom competition. (Express & Echo)

Green fingers won the day at Exmouth Garden Club's Annual Show, held at the town's Elizabeth Hall, 25 June 1988. Making the presentations to the winners was Barry Willoughby, the chairman of Exmouth Garden Club committee. (Express & Echo)

Work is well under way on a major scheme to create a new indoor leisure pool at Devon Cliffs Holiday Park at Sandy Bay, near Exmouth, 22 February 1988. This covered swimming pool was part of an on-going programme of improvements at the holiday park by Haven Leisure, the owners. The pool work was carried out by the Exmouth building company Greenaways, and was completed in time for the camp opening at Easter that year. (Express & Echo)

With the opening of the new town-centre Bejam store on 14 December 1988 twenty new jobs were created in Honiton. The shop was in Lace Walk, and the Mayor and Mayoress were on hand for the official ceremony. Pictured at the opening are, left to right: the new store manager Mark Wood, Bejam regional director Roger Price, Honiton town crier Joe Lake, the Mayor, -?- and the Mayoress. (Express & Echo)

John Yallop (left), the curator of the Allhallows Museum in Honiton, is seen here on 26 October 1990 receiving a gift to the museum from Robert and Barbara Davidson, formerly of the town's Angel Hotel. They presented to Mr Yallop the Honiton coat of arms and a framed history of the town that had been displayed in the bar of the hotel. (Express & Echo)

Ron Gigg, the chairman of East Devon District Council, lays the foundation stone at the Dunning Court project, Honiton, 14 February 1989. Frank Lock, the chairman of the Housing Committee, is standing on his right. (Express & Echo)

A pleasant ceremony in Honiton on the last day of March 1990. The Mayor of Honiton Bob Walker and the twinning association president Pat Allen are seen welcoming their German guests from Honiton's twin town of Gronau, who were led by Eckhard Grastore. (Express & Echo)

June 1988 saw the 300-year anniversary of the founding of Ottery St Mary United Reformed Church. One of the events was a performance of a drama-documentary written by Don Quantill of Feniton, re-enacting the period when this church was struggling to become established in the town and showing the persecution suffered by those involved. With Don Quantill are members of the cast: Jonathan Hounslow as Thomas Quinton, Jennifer Mackie as Patience Quinton, Gwen Tilt as Mistress Quinton and David Air as Thomas Axe. (Express & Echo)

Colyford church centenary service and dedication, 17 January 1989. The Dean of Exeter the Revd Richard Eyres and the vicar of Colyton and Colyford the Revd David Gunn-Johnson are seen outside the church before the service and the dedication of the new church gate in memory of Frank and Alma Hawkes. The couple had lived in the village for many years and Frank was a popular former mayor of the Borough of Colyford, who worked hard for the good of the village. (Express & Echo)

Service awards were made to Joan and Bill Drew and Mary Davey by the Beer Regatta Committee on 14 October 1987. Joan and Bill Drew, sitting on the left, were retiring from the Regatta Committee after serving for twenty-five years. Mary Davey, on the right, had served as the secretary and was continuing on the committee. Her award was given in recognition of her work over the years. Beer Regatta Princess of that year Lynne Beavis is standing centre back with her attendants Elaine Baker, left, and Tracey Hawker. (Express & Echo)

Seaton Town Council certainly dropped a clanger when they commissioned a Plymouth art student to design a sculpture to stand on Seaton seafront. In the photograph above, East Devon District Council's chairman Bill Thorne has climbed on a wall to try to placate the outraged crowd after the work was revealed, March 1991. Following a petition to have the monstrosity removed, the statue was taken down on 22 April 1991. In the photograph below, John While, Michael O'Sullivan and Arthur Smith drink a toast as the Seaton sculpture finally leaves the seafront for a place in some distant theme park. It is said on good authority that this piece is now worth much more than the original price – there must be a moral in this saga. (Express & Echo)

Exmouth floods, 28 September–6 October 1960. Following an unusually wet summer, the last week of September was one of almost continuous rain. During the night of Thursday, 29 September the exceptional downpour flooded the Withycombe Brook. The rain continued the following morning and by midday storm water caused the brook to overflow, resulting in severe flooding in the Exeter Road area. Muddy water up to 4 ft deep poured into houses, causing much damage to furniture and carpets. During the following days help came from the fire brigade, the Royal Marines at Lympstone, the Wessex Brigade from Exeter and the Durhams, who were stationed at Honiton. Unfortunately, no sooner had the mess been cleared up than the whole chain of events was repeated. During the evening of Thursday, 6 October a thunderstorm accompanied by 2 hours of heavy rain caused flooding in the area again. This time it was more severe, with at least 1,000 homes affected and once more voluntary workers, firemen, police and troops rushed in to help. The photograph above shows Exeter Road under water during the floods, while in the photograph below, the local Renault garage is partially submerged by flood water. Note the Army lorry assisting with the clean-up. (*Seaton Museum*)

On 6 May 1935 the whole country united to acclaim King George V when he celebrated the Silver Jubilee of his reign. Through vast crowds of cheering people King George and Queen Mary drove to St Paul's for the thanksgiving service. Throughout the country the weather was perfect and the King, whose devotion to duty earned him the respect of the whole nation, was overcome at the reception that he received. Looking back at that event nearly seventy years ago, you are left with the impression that the Jubilee was extremely well organised. It had been a wonderful day, although one journalist did make the comment that Jubilee night was going to be responsible for a large harvest of Jubilee babies. In the photograph above, flags and bunting are the order of the day in Fore Street. In the photograph below, the people of Seaton gather on the seafront for a thanksgiving service. (*Ted Gosling Collection*)

Originally named Pit Bottom, the old farmhouse of Fancy Farm in the village of Dunkeswell must have witnessed many strange sights during its 400-year-plus lifetime, but none quite so odd as the one seen here in 1968. These musicians were members of an 'underground' music movement, who played in a band called Mousetrap. They stayed at Fancy Farm with Ted Gosling, who then owned the property, for six months, making a record, and on the day they played outside complaints about the noise came from over 2 miles away. The underground music movement, or 'post-Punk', began as a response to the big-budget, over-produced music of that period. The bands avoided major record labels in pursuit of artistic freedom. Ted never found out what became of them, but there was an underground music band called Mousetrap who produced two records in the USA in 1990. (*Ted Gosling Collection*)

A sad day for the workers at Beswicks in January 1986. This company manufactured electrical circuits in Victoria Road, Exmouth. At the time of this photograph the staff had just received notice that the business was to close, and they were soon to lose their jobs. (Express & Echo)

The Sidmouth College team that participated in the Ten Tors event, May 2000. Ten Tors is an annual competition held in May in which teams of up to six young people visit ten Dartmoor Tors on one of three different length routes, between 35 and 55 miles. They spend one night camping on the moor and use their navigational skills to complete their route successfully. It was very hot in May 2000 and many of the competing teams retired through dehydration. The Sidmouth College team successfully completed the 35-mile route, and are seen here being congratulated on their achievement. Helen Ing from Beer was the only girl in this team. (*Helen Ing*)

The unveiling of the commemorative Beer stone which marked the re-opening of the quarries, *c.* 1990. This stone was the first to be brought out when quarrying restarted and stands in the lower car park at Beer. Left to right: Trevor Poole, Amey Road Stone Company manager, Mike Green, Philip Batstone, Alf Boalch. (Express & Echo)

East Devon's carnivals are important features in the regional calendar. Before the carnivals can take place a great deal of time and care is spent by the various committees in preparing for the event. They all deserve our praise, our congratulations and our heartfelt thanks for keeping the traditions of carnival alive. In the photograph on the left, Ted Gosling is crowning 'Miss Seaton', the 1993 Seaton Carnival Queen. In the photograph on the right, the 1st Ottery St Mary Beaver Scouts take part in the Ottery St Mary Carnival procession as a walking group of warriors, *c.* 1997. (*Left: Ted Gosling Collection; right: Colin Bowerman*)

Opposite, above: More than 300 runners set off from The Esplanade at Seaton at the start of the annual 5-mile fun run organised by the Axe Valley Round Table, 15 April 1986. It was the third race the Round Table had staged, and entries were up by about a hundred compared with the previous year. They also hoped to improve on the 1985 sponsorship total of £2,500. (Express & Echo)

Opposite, below: 'My turn next, please.' – Major Howard Floyd of the Army Air Corps at the Branscombe Air Show with Natasha and Ayesha Simmons, 26 July 1992. (Express & Echo)

Ted Gosling in his 1924 vintage two-seater Bullnose Morris, with friend Charles Kenlock in the passenger seat, August 1960. They were taking part in a vintage car rally at Bere Regis. He attended many rallies with this car, including the parade of vehicles at the opening of the new National Motor Museum at Beaulieu. In 1958, at a rally at which over 500 surviving Bullnose Morris cars were present, he met Lord Nuffield, the founder of the Morris car factory. The Austin 7 following on behind was an early example of the 'baby Austin' model, dating back to 1923, the year they first went on sale. (*Ted Gosling Collection*)

Knocking down a pile of pennies collected for charity in the old Working Men's Club, Market Street, Exmouth, *c.* 1955. (*Ted Gosling Collection*)

A tense moment in Honiton High Street during December 1992. Honiton Market is always held in the High Street on a Tuesday, but these traders had illegally set up stalls on a Thursday. East Devon District Council acted very quickly and the police were directed to move them on. (Express & Echo)

Margaret Thatcher, then Prime Minister, reading the 'riot act' to cattle at a farm in Colyton during a visit to East Devon, 18 April 1986. (Express & Echo)

The big event for celebration in East Devon in 1937 was the Coronation of King George VI on 12 May. Although the monarchy had gone through a bad time, with the recent abdication of King Edward VIII, the new king had already won the affection of his subjects since his accession in December 1936, and there was enormous rejoicing throughout the country as Coronation day approached. The weather that day was unkind and it opened with a cold, grey morning, although the situation did improve later on. Every town and village in East Devon had formed a committee to make arrangements for the great day, and streets everywhere were lavishly decorated. A full programme of events was organised, which included a church service, sports, dancing and street parties. The schoolchildren were given special Coronation mugs, which were attractive souvenirs, unlike the poorly designed mugs given out to some of East Devon's children for the millennium. In this picture, Clifford Charles Gould, Chairman of Seaton Urban District Council, is seen, spade in hand, planting an oak tree on the corner of Old Beer Road, Seaton, to commemorate the Coronation. The author knows most of the children because he was with them on that special day, and he is pleased to report that the oak tree is still there. It deserves a plaque to inform people today why it was planted. (*Ted Gosling Collection*)

The post-war gloom in Britain was temporarily lifted by the Festival of Britain. The central feature of this festival was the South Bank Exhibition, on the south bank of the river near Waterloo station. It was an immediate success and people flocked to it in their thousands. Events were held nationwide in commemoration of Prince Albert's Exhibition of 1851, and to demonstrate Britain's economic recovery. The Festival of Britain was opened by King George VI from the steps of St Paul's on 3 May 1951. Celebrations were held that day throughout East Devon, and I was the organising secretary of the day's proceedings in Seaton. One of the highlights of that day was the pyramid display given by the youth club on Seaton seafront. In the photograph above, the youth club team is seen, left to right: Derek Real, Derek Jones, Brian Steele, Alan Baker, Brian Davis, Edward Cockram, -?-, Dick Moore, Don Rogers. In the photograph below, the team demonstrate their skills watched by the admiring crowd. (*Brian Steele*)

Meet of the Axe Vale Harriers at the White Hart, Colyford, *c.* 1900. They met two days a week to hunt foxes and hares, with a season from the middle of September through to the middle of April. *(Ted Gosling Collection)*

Competitors in a bicycle race at a flower show and fête in Axminster, *c.* 1906. As they prepare for the starting flag, the riders have grim determination written all over their faces – it is not clear whether their assistants were there to give the cyclists a push start, or just to hold the cycles steady. *(Norman Lambert)*

The most renowned of all the events that take place in East Devon during the summer months must be the Sidmouth International Folk Festival, which attracts dancing groups, musicians and tourists from all over the world during the first week in August. It was in 1955 that the English Folk Dance and Song Society first came to Sidmouth to perform, and from small beginnings this event has grown to the size it is today. Musicians and dancers can be seen all over the town, providing free entertainment to appreciative audiences, with the Arena stage at Knowle putting on a varied programme. In the photograph above, a Maori dance troupe perform at the Knowle Arena during the 1995 Sidmouth Festival, which was thoroughly enjoyed by a large audience. In the photograph below, in the same year, an American step dance group can be seen going through a lively dance routine. (*Colin Bowerman*)

Robin Barnard, secretary of the Seaton Hospital League of Friends, receiving a cheque for the hospital from Colyton Carnival Queen, May 1994. (Express & Echo)

Opposite, above: The commemoration of the fiftieth anniversary of VE Day outside Colyton town hall, 8 May 1995. To these Colyton children, VE Day was an event in history that their grandparents sometimes talked about, a day on which, they were often told, the whole country had joined together in celebrating Victory in Europe, but an occasion such as this must have helped them to realise what this day meant in 1945. (*John Lavers/Seaton Museum*)

Opposite, below: The laying of the foundation stone of the Axminster Cottage Hospital, Chard Street, September 1910. This was carried out by Mr Cornish, and the hospital was officially opened on 18 June 1912. (*Norman Lambert*)

The locomotive *Seaton* was a light Pacific of the West Country class, number 21C120. The naming ceremony of this fine engine, seen here in pristine condition, took place at Seaton Junction on 25 June 1946. In 1968 the name-plate was presented by British Railways to Seaton Urban District Council to keep for the people of Seaton. The Council, much to their shame, failed to appreciate its great monetary and historical value, and through downright carelessness managed to lose it. Considering its size, this must have been quite difficult to do, and it brings to mind that wonderful Devonshire expression 'they couldn't organise a booze-up in a pub'. (*Ted Gosling Collection*)

Interior view of Nestles Munitions Factory, Branscombe, *c.* 1943. With the outbreak of the Second World War, Sydney Pritchard and his brother William won a Government contract. Their factory in Holloway, North London, was moved to a garage in The Square, Branscombe. From this secret site the company turned out millions of shell fuses and aircraft components, but was never a target for German bombers. Much credit must go to William and Sydney Pritchard who, with their workers, played an important role in the war effort. (*Ted Gosling Collection*)

Just a few days before the advent of the new millennium the Axe Valley Heritage Association commissioned local photographer Chris Byrne-Jones to take a group photograph of its members to commemorate the occasion, and here on a cold December day approaching the end of 1999 they assembled for this. Just over 2,000 years ago a new hope entered the world with the birth of Jesus and Christianity survived against all the odds to reach the twentieth century, the atomic age and the new millennium. This was welcomed by a firework party that lit up the whole world, and across Britain a chain of beacons symbolically linked the country. Throughout East Devon the night sky was transformed by starbursts of pink, silver and gold as rockets were launched with spectacular effect, and at the stroke of midnight from Big Ben thousands of people danced, sang and hugged each other. (*Axe Valley Heritage Association*)

ACKNOWLEDGEMENTS

I am grateful to the many people who have contributed material for this book. Particular thanks must go to the editor of the *Express & Echo* for allowing me to use photographs from the paper's archives. Thanks are also due to Chris Wright, without whose help this book would not have been possible.

I am indebted to Norman Lambert for allowing me to use photographs from his wonderful postcard collection, and to Colin Bowerman for the kindness shown to me when he produced much needed images to complete various chapters.

Special thanks must go to the following people, without whose photographs and advice this book would not have been possible: John Stoodley, Daphne Harman Young, the Joslin family, Alex Alexander, Seaton Museum, Mike Clement, Holly Ford from Honiton, Terry Scales, Ann Spencer, Julie Rowe, Margaret Rogers, Nigel Albright, Helen Ing, Philip Higginson, Sheila Luxton, Devon Wildlife Trust, Brian Steele, Ann Adams and Meadows Estate Agents. Thanks must also go to Simon Fletcher of Sutton Publishing for his assistance, and to Roy Chapple.

I am grateful to my wife Carol for her encouragement and assistance, and to Lyn Marshall, who gave invaluable help in producing this book.

Many books, newspapers and organisations were consulted, too many to mention, but the following were a mine of information: *Express & Echo*, Pulman's *Weekly News*, *Devon* by W.G. Hoskins, *The Village School* by June Lewis, *Seventy Summers* by Tony Harman, *A Country Camera* by Gordon Winter, Seaton Tramway, Manor House School, *Colyton Grammar School* by Gerald Gosling and Peco.